Since Concern was founded in 1968 our aim has been to improve the lives of the poorest people on the planet. People who go to bed hungry each night, people with little access to safe water, healthcare or schooling and people who in times of crises or natural disaster are most at risk of losing the few possessions they own.

Today Concern Worldwide is one of the world's most respected international NGOs, working with over 500 partners in 27 countries throughout the developing world. We listen to the very poorest people, they know more about poverty, disease and discrimination than anyone else and armed with that knowledge we under-take long term development work and respond to emergency situations as they arise.

We place immense importance on working with individuals, communities and local government's and we empower people to develop the best and most sustainable solutions that work for them.

In the face of unacceptable poverty and the denial of basic human rights our campaign and advocacy work brings our experience to the highest levels of decision and policy making. We aim to give the poorest of the poor a voice, knowing that justice on a global level demands that they be heard and respected.

"MR SECRETARY-GENERAL, LADIES AND GENTLEMEN ..."

The Concern Worldwide 2010 Writing Competition

Edited by
Michael Doorly

The Liffey Press

Published by
The Liffey Press
Ashbrook House, 10 Main Street
Raheny, Dublin 5, Ireland
www.theliffeypress.com

A catalogue record of this book is
available from the British Library.

ISBN 978-1-905785-83-4 (pbk)

Illustrations by Conor Gallagher

Printed in Ireland by Colour Books.

Contents

Acknowledgements xi

Foreword
Tom Arnold xiii

Preface
Michael Doorly xv

"Human Chain", a poem
Seamus Heaney xvii

Part 1
JUNIOR CATEGORY
(12–15 years old)

First Place
Megan Ross 3

Second Place
Rory Copeland 6

Third Place
Ciara O'Sullivan 10

Shortlist
Arun Murtagh 13
Makinde Oluwadamilola 16
Zoe Hayes 19
Ciara Moloney 23
Eibhlin Lonergan 25
Matthew Salit 28
Hannah Heeran 32
Emma McLaughlin 35

Contents

Passages, Extracts, Quotes

Mark McDermott 41
Sophie Poll 43
Ciara Kelleher 45
Rosin Lonergan 47
Megan Carey 48
Orla O'Gorman 50
Alyah Ali 51
James Trouton 53
Stephen Conn 55
Emma Rutter 57
Orla Lenehen 59
Deirbhile Craven 61
Aditi Upmanyu 62
Iona Teague 64
Eimear Duff 65
Jennifer Gaule 67
Corey McClean 69
Lucy Dudman 70
Kelly Skillen 71
Amy Tate 72
Mohammed Ali Anasov 74
Aisling Taylor 75
Mark Stewart 76
Ellie Collett 77
Toni Upton 78

Soundbites

Eireann Moloney 80
Nathan Murray 81
Martha Glaser 81
Dáire Brown 82
Sharon Greaney 83
Eimear Millane 83
Pierce Cambay 84
Sarah Apsey 85
Aimee Kerr 85
Dayna Devlin 86

Contents

Part 2
SENIOR CATEGORY
(16–18 years old)

First Place
Emer Jones 89

Second Place
Peadar O'Lamhna 94

Joint Third Place
Sarah Foley 99

Joint Third Place
Nancy Jane Carragher 104

Shortlist
Naoise Dolan 109
Paul Kelly 113
Lucy Jones 118
Annie Clarke 121
Maria McWalter 125
Jennifer Kinsella 129

Passages, Extracts, Quotes
Gabrielle O'Donoghue 133
Vu Lan Nguyen 135
Jessica Maguire 137
Eimear Cleary 139
Dara Jones 141
Shane McKenna 143
Ashling Flanagan 146
Claire Benson 148
Roisin Ryan 149
Stephanie Reid 152
Michelle Joyce 154
Caoimhe Ní Chorcora 156
Robert Bolton 157
Niamh Brady 160
Mairead O'Sullivan 162
Grace Kevaney 164

Contents

Sarah Bradley 166
Colm Lawless 168
Robert Boland.. 171
Shikha Shahi 173

Soundbites
Carol Shanley 175
Alyssa Liljequist.. 175
Niamh Heavey 177
Jin Rui Yap.. 177
Daniel McFadden... 177
Helen Dinan.. 178
Aisling McGing... 179
Jessica Earl 179
Cara Halliday 180
Stephanie Okolo.. 181

Part 3
ADULT CATEGORY
(over 19 years old)

First Place
Gerard Foley.. 185

Second Place
Flynn Coleman 190

Third Place
Margaret Casserly.. 195

Shortlist
Brian Harding.. 200
Ndifor Elves Funnui.. 205
Joanna John... 209
Thandazile Mpofu 212
Yvonne Campbell 217
Elizabeth Doane 221
Sounmitra Subinaya 225

Contents

Passages, Extracts, Quotes

Ibn Garba Safiya...229

Nicholas Santizo 230

Dashell Yancha..234

Meenakshi Roy...237

Soundbites

Arvind Kumar Apsingikar..240

Tara Finglas 240

Innocent Chidi Iskiakpu 241

Cathy Howlett..241

Mary Wall 242

Abra Wagdi 242

Catherine Conlon...243

Colm Turner 244

Peter McCarron..244

Tom Smith 245

Irene Chikumbo 245

List of Participating Schools..247

Millennium Development Goals (MDGs)

To be achieved by 2015

Goal 1	Eradicate Extreme Poverty and Hunger
Goal 2	Achieve Universal Primary Education
Goal 3	Promote Gender Equality and Empower Women
Goal 4	Reduce Child Mortality
Goal 5	Improve Maternal Health
Goal 6	Combat HIV and AIDS, Malaria and Other Diseases
Goal 7	Ensure Environmental Sustainability
Goal 8	Develop a Global Partnership for Development

"No country genuinely committed to good governance and economic reform should miss out on achieving the MDGs through lack of finance."

Monterrey Financing for Development
Conference, March 2002

Acknowledgements

Concern expresses its sincere thanks and appreciation to the hundreds of people who entered the third annual Concern Writing Competition. We were delighted to receive over 650 entries from 26 countries around the world, and we were even more delighted to read the quality, sincerity and passion that went into each and every entry.

Our thanks are also due to the many people who served as first round judges for their diligence and hard work in reading each entry not just once but twice, and in so doing ensuring that every 'speech' was given the best possible chance of reaching the final stages.

Our panel of final round judges included Mr. Hans Zomer, the Director of Dochas, the Irish Network of Development NGOs; Mr. David Joyce, Equality Officer with the Irish Congress of Trade Unions; Mr Johnny Sheehan, Development Education Co-ordinator with the National Youth Council of Ireland; and Mr John O'Connor and Mrs Kelly McShane, Board Members of Concern USA.

We owe a special thank you to the Concern IT department and in particular Ellen Ward, Graham Coogan, Barry Gildea and Vincent Richardson for ensuring that all of the links, forms and uploads worked so well, and to Ruth Rowan, Naoise Kavanagh, Alan O'Reilly and Niall Ó Murchú, for keeping the competition 'web enabled'.

David Givens from The Liffey Press is the essence of grace under pressure and we are particularly grateful for his patience and calm, and thanks as well to Sinead McKenna for her design work and creativity.

We must also acknowledge the work of Evanna Craig and Grainne O'Brien from the Concern Active Citizenship Unit for their work in uploading the entries, recruiting judges and ensuring that all aspects of the competition ran according to plan.

Finally, to Eimear Rigby and Michael Commane in the Concern Communications Unit we owe our thanks for helping to spread the good word.

Foreword

Tom Arnold, CEO, Concern Worldwide

Over the past ten years there has been progress in working towards the Millennium Development Goals (MDGs) which have achieved tangible benefits for millions of the world's poorest and most vulnerable people in alleviating poverty, increasing access to education, improving women's health and reducing disease. That progress toward achieving them, in the words of the current United Nations Secretary General, has been "unacceptably slow", or that the global economic crisis has further reduced the prospects of their achievement, is to recognise that huge efforts must still be made by governments and citizens across the globe if these goals are to be met.

Setting broad, ambitious goals is not new to the United Nations. The eradication of smallpox, efforts at conflict resolution and the introduction of groundbreaking human rights treaties are testaments to the good that can be unleashed when member nations work together for the advancement of all the world's citizens. Within this context, the MDGs are the most broadly supported, comprehensive and specific development goals the world has ever agreed upon and they represent a major global opportunity for saving lives, protecting freedoms and creating peace.

In the introduction to the Millennium Development Goals Report 2010, Ban Ki Moon reminds us yet again that: "the world possesses the resources and knowledge to ensure that even the poorest countries, and others held back by disease, geographic isolation or civil strife, can be empowered to achieve the MDGs. Meeting the goals is everyone's business."

And because they are "everyone's business" I am delighted that so many people took part in this year's Concern Writing Competition where we asked entrants to send us the speech they would deliver to the United Nations MDG Summit in September 2010. What comes across time and again in so many of the "speeches" is that the MDGs are achievable, but there is clearly an urgent need to address challenges, acknowledge failures and come together to overcome the obstacles to their achievement. It is not a new message – in fact, it is a message world leaders have heard many times before – but with just five years to go before the 2015 deadline it is one that must not only be heard but delivered on as well.

Preface

Michael Doorly

The third annual Concern Writing Competition challenged entrants to send us the speech that they would deliver to the United Nations General Assembly on the Millennium Development Goals (MDGs). As in the previous two years of the competition we were hugely impressed with the number (nearly 700) and quality of the entries as well as the growing geographical reach of the competition (26 countries).

Whether those who sent us their speeches had any previous knowledge of the MDGs, whether they knew that the world had made eight solemn promises to its poorest and most vulnerable citizens in the year 2000 and whether they knew that there are just five years left before those promises are to be delivered, is not important. What is important is the clear sense of injustice and even outrage that comes through in so many of the speeches, that countless lives are ruined or lost not because of a lack of resources but because of a lack of political will.

To agree to judge such a competition is to commit to a lengthy and demanding process. The words of Hans Zomer, a member of this year's judging panel, clearly captures the difficulty faced by each of the judges: *"It was far from easy to make decisions about which speech to rank the highest. Many of them employed a great deal of creativity and used very different and effective approaches to deliver a great speech. However it seems that there is an unspoken belief among many of the contributors that 'the UN' must act whereas a key message and challenge of development is that people themselves must be empowered to take control of their lives. "*

That so many people took the time and effort to put into words their solidarity and hope for the world's poorest people makes running such a competition truly worthwhile. The challenge of course is to ensure that these words are heard at the highest levels and that they are translated into long lasting and sustained action.

We have reproduced in full the winning and shortlisted speeches from this year's competition and have included edited extracts from over 100 other entrants. It is our hope that by presenting a copy of this book to An Taoiseach Mr Brian Cowen that he along with leaders from all United Nations member states will know that not only is there support for any actions they may take to reach the MDGs but there is a firm expectation that they will do all in their power to fulfill them.

Human Chain

By Seamus Heaney

Seeing the bags of meal passed hand to hand
In close-up by the aid workers, and soldiers
Firing over the mob, I was braced again

With the grip on two sack corners,
Two packed wads I had worked to lugs
To give me purchase, ready for the heave

The eye-to-eye, one-two, one-two upswing
On to the trailer, then the stoop and drag and drain
Of the next lift. Nothing surpassed

That quick unburdening, backbreaks's truest payback,
A letting go which will not come again,
Or it will, once. And for all.

Nobel Laureate Seamus Heaney has been a long-term supporter of Concern and is a patron of Concern US. Reprinted with permission of the author.

Part One

JUNIOR CATEGORY

(12–15 years old)

Extract from the Millennium Declaration,

United Nations, September, 2000

Development and Poverty Eradication

... We will spare no effort to free our fellow men, women and children from the abject and dehumanizing conditions of extreme poverty, to which more than a billion of them are currently subjected. We are committed to making the right to development a reality for everyone, and to freeing the entire human race from want.

...We resolve, therefore, to create an environment — at the national and global levels alike — which is conducive to development and to the elimination of poverty.

... Success in meeting these objectives depends, inter alia, on good governance within each country. It also depends on good governance at the international level, and on transparency in the financial, monetary and trading systems. We are committed to an open, equitable, rule-based, predictable and non-discriminatory multilateral trading and financial system.

First Place – Junior

Megan Ross

St Joseph of Cluny Secondary School, Killiney, Co Dublin, Ireland, Age 15

MDG 3 – Promote Gender Equality and Empower Women

Mr. President, Mr. Secretary-General, Ladies and Gentlemen,

Ten years ago you or, as the case may be, your predecessors, sat down together at the Millennium Summit and you made me a promise. You promised me that by 2015, I would be living in a world that doesn't see in blue and pink, but sees every single one of us as the equally valuable human beings that we are and always will be. You promised me a life where my gender will not impede or hinder my ability to become successful in whatever it is I choose to do with it and will instead empower me to live it to its full potential. You promised me that the world will be, by 2015, one where the fact that I am a girl will never be something to be ashamed of but rather something to celebrate every single day I am one. You made this promise to me, my mother, my sister and every single other female human being on Earth.

You also made this promise to Malenga. She's eight years old and lives in Malawi. She has two older sisters and a twin brother. This year Malenga had to stop going to school. She didn't understand why her brother could continue going and she couldn't, so she asked her father. He told her that they couldn't afford to send both of them to school anymore, so they sent her brother. Boys need to go to school because they need to get a job when they grow up. Malenga was confused because she thought that girls could get jobs too. Her father laughed, telling her that her job would be raising her family, because her husband certainly wouldn't know how to do that. All Malenga needed to know she could learn from her mother and sisters, at home. Malenga doesn't understand why things are the way they are, but she must accept that she'll never be anything more than a housewife. That's a harsh reality for any eight-year-old to have presented to her. With no education, it *is* her reality.

An education opens up doors to people, doors which will lead them out of poverty – doors which will remain closed forever if they are discriminated against over something as meaningless as the configuration of their chromosomes. When little girls like Malenga are denied an equal opportunity to go to school, they may be losing out on learning many important lessons but they definitely do learn one: they do not matter as much as boys. When little boys like Malenga's brother are allowed to go to school and their sisters are left at home, they too are learning a lesson: they are more important than girls. It may be difficult to alter the attitudes and beliefs of adults, who've lived their entire lives accepting the exclusion of women as a social norm, but we're certainly not doing anyone any favours if we allowed them to be passed on to their children when they're at their most impressionable. These children are the future of these nations – they're the ones upon whom the real, long-term change on all fronts relies. That change won't happen if only the boys get a chance to reach their potential, and if girls are let believe that they don't matter.

The target you set was to eliminate gender disparity in primary and secondary education, preferably by 2005, and in all levels of education no later than 2015. Despite the obvious importance of ensuring that every child has an equal opportunity to receive an education, gender parity still does not exist in primary and secondary education, five years after you said it would. To quote from the Millennium Development Goals Report 2009, "In 2007, only 53 of the 171 countries with available data had achieved gender parity ... in both primary and secondary education". That figure shows an increase of 14 countries since 1999. At the current rate of progress, we're looking at 67 countries having achieved gender parity in primary and secondary education by 2015 and 171 countries by, wait for it, 2071. By that stage it's unlikely Malenga will even be around to appreciate your work.

More needs to be done to create societies where women can achieve just as much as men – so parents can see that their daughter has as much potential as their son, that her education is just as valuable as his. More needs to be done to provide funding for schools – so that parents won't have to choose which child to send to school and which to keep at home in the first place. More needs to be done to eliminate gender inequality, to seal up the cracks before Malenga and all the thousands of girls just like her can fall through them. More needs to be done and it needs to be done now.

It's 2010 now and time is running out. Running out, but not gone yet. It's time to get your act together and realise that you have the power to make a difference. Don't you dream of a world where a child like Malenga, whose family has practically nothing, could go on to make something better of herself? She may not grow up to be a powerful politician, but you never know, maybe her granddaughter or great-granddaughter will. By giving Malenga an education, you're putting her in a position to provide even more for her children and for them to do the same for theirs.

Words whisper, actions shout; right now all I can hear are whispers. Girls like Malenga need you to shout for them – they have no voice. Gender equality cannot and will not happen overnight, but as Confucius said, "A journey of a thousand miles starts with a single step". It's your job to take that step, but with every step you take, more girls will be able to walk with you, on the journey to a better world for us all.

SECOND PLACE – JUNIOR

Rory Copeland

Methodist College, Belfast,
Northern Ireland, Age 14

MDG 8 – DEVELOP A GLOBAL PARTNERSHIP FOR DEVELOPMENT

Mr. President, Mr. Secretary-General, Ladies and Gentlemen,

My name is Rory Copeland, and I am a pupil at Methodist College Belfast. I am here to address you on the eighth Millennium Development Goal: to develop a global partnership for development. Leaders, the day I started primary school, 8 September 2000, was the day on which you adopted the Millennium Declaration. The world in which we live has changed dramatically in the ten years since then, but the Millennium Development Goals remain the same, and so too should our promise to fulfil them by the year 2015. To develop a global partnership for development means that we must work as a team to make the trading system fairer, help with debt cancellation, and bring technology to more of the world's poorest countries. I believe that global partnership is one of the most important Millennium Development Goals, as it has a direct effect on all of the others.

Unfortunately, much of what I have heard and read in the ten years since 2000 is evidence of the world's continued lack of unity. Wars in Iraq and Afghanistan tear the lives of the people apart. Outside of China, the number of people living in poverty has actually risen from 1990 to 2005 by 36 million. This figure is expected to increase still. Why? A rise in food and fuel prices, followed by a global economic crisis beyond all reckoning, in 2008, has brought to light the weaknesses in our global partnership. The poorer countries in the world were worst hit, as aid donations fell, and poverty and hunger took hold once again. To make matters worse, 2010 brought earthquakes in Haiti, Chile and Turkey, and aid is now needed more than ever. It is shocking, therefore, to see the G20 leaders discussing banking bonuses at the summit last year in Pittsburgh, when, because of their lack of foresight, the lives of billions of people around the world have sunk deeper into poverty and misery.

Since 2000, steps have been taken to create greater global partnership, and we have seen improvements. In 2005, leaders, at the Gleneagles Summit, you agreed to raise the amount of aid given to the poorer countries from $80 billion to $130 billion by 2010. Because some of the aid pledged was as a percentage of gross national income, the real amount of money being given may drop by a sum of billions because of the global recession. We must therefore work harder under pressure to ensure that the targets are met!

One of the main principles of global partnership should be the equality of all nations, and we can only achieve this by ensuring that disadvantaged countries, such as small island developing states and landlocked countries, should receive more favourable trade subsidies. Governments of developed countries should not be allowed to subsidise their farmers, so that farmers in poorer countries can't sell their crops on the international market. Finance must not be totally controlled by the wealthy nations of the globe; it must be beneficial to the whole world.

Another problem that has blocked the path to a fairer world is the repayment of debt. Members of the United Nations, imagine having to let your own children starve because you have to give all the money you earn to your landlord. This is the problem that the governments of many less developed countries face today, trying to repay wealthier countries and having to leave their own people without food and water. The only solution to this problem is for more countries to cancel the debt of the world's poorest nations. In addition, let us all support the efforts of the poorer countries by buying their goods, and so giving work to their young people. These countries' exports had increased, but, sadly, have now fallen again because of the financial crisis.

In the wealthier countries in the world, technology has changed our lives dramatically. I believe that the same technology can greatly change the lives of the people in the rest of the world. From 2002 to 2007, the number of people to have internet access around the world has increased from 11 per cent to 21 per cent. However, only 1.5 per cent of people in the least developed countries are connected to the internet. Technology will attract international business and will create jobs for the local people. Families living in the most disaster-stricken parts of the world will be able to access vital information, and charities around the world will be able to respond much more quickly.

The one thing I believe the world needs more now than ever before is responsible leadership to promote global partnership. Leaders who have experience and wisdom, who won't fight for their own gain, but for the good of the whole world. Leaders who will inspire the world economic powers to make sacrifices. Leaders who will not falter under pressure. You, the members of the United Nations, are the leaders of today.

The global community has a steep and slippery slope to climb to reach true, fair global partnership. There will be setbacks, and disaster will strike, but we must not let these stop us from reaching the top of the mountain. In your time as leaders of the United Nations, you have shown that you can guide the world up this slippery slope. I urge you to keep climbing, and to ensure that the whole world follows. Remember, we must hang together, or be hanged separately!

In 2015, when I leave school, I hope the Millennium Development Goals will have been fulfilled. But by the New York Summit in September I ask you to carry out these goals: provide trade subsidies, cancel any debts you can, and support technologies for the world's poorest countries. But most of all, honour your commitments to meet your aid targets. You promised to go one mile – now you must go two!

THIRD PLACE – JUNIOR

Ciara O'Sullivan

Loreto Secondary School,
Fermoy, Co. Cork, Ireland
Age 15

MDG 5 – IMPROVE MATERNAL HEALTH

Mr. President, Mr. Secretary-General, Ladies and Gentlemen, my name is Ciara O'sullivan and I would like to thank the UN Secretary-General, Ban Ki Moon, for extending an invitation to me to speak here today. As all of us here today know, we have five years to complete the goals which you promised to complete in 2000. I am sure that as you signed that piece of paper that you were filled with the same sense of hope, the same yearning as I feel now. Perhaps as the years passed by this hope has slowly lost its initial spark and the flame has slowly died out. Perhaps we have forgotten the purpose for which we signed that piece of paper. Today we must restore that hope. We must improve the world with a new zest and energy. We must make the world a better place for all its citizens.

A goal which I feel is particularly important is improving maternal health. In 2000, 189 of you pledged to reduce by three-quarters the death rate of women in childbirth. By 2005 it had been reduced by only 1 per cent. This is a disgrace! Every year half a million women die in childbirth. As we sit here comfortably for an hour, 500 African women will have lost their babies. And this is due to the lack of easily provided medical supplies! As

10

Doctor Grace Kondiugo of Chad said: "When a woman becomes pregnant she has one foot in the grave."

I believe that the deaths of these women are however too often thought of as a statistic. Each mother or child that dies is not just another number to be added to a chart; it is the death of a person, a person who has the same hopes and fears and dreams as all of us here today.

Many people regard the day that they receive a child as one of the happiest in their lives. Women in Sub-Saharan Africa live in fear of that day. Imagine for a moment a soon-to-be mother. She sits for months dreaming of the beautiful child she will give birth to, planning its life, excitement and anticipation lighting her eyes. She longs for the day when she can finally hold the child she has been carrying for nine months. Is there anything more beautiful? Her counterpart in Africa knows that her life is at risk, she knows that out of 22 women giving birth she could be the one to die. She knows how excruciatingly painful the procedure will be as she has probably been circumcised. Even imagining a happy life for her child would be foolishly optimistic. I ask you, how can we allow this to happen? How can we allow such needless suffering to continue?

Any effort against poverty starts with women and children. Women play a vital role in the development of an economy. Studies state that it is preferable to educate women as they pass this knowledge to their children and communities, educating those around them. It is also shown that the more female members there are in a government the lower the rate of corruption such as in Rwanda. When women play such a vital role in our society and hugely contribute to helping lessen poverty, how can we allow them to die of easily preventable diseases during pregnancy and during childbirth? If a child's mother dies while giving birth that child will subsequently have little social schooling and will have lived much of its life in poverty. This leads to a greater probability of crime and prostitution. If we do not act this will be the generation of the future.

Medical supplies must be made more readily available in the third world. Many women die of diseases such as eclampsia which can be prevented by magnesium sulphate – a drug hardly the cost of table salt! In 2003 and 2004 the world spent at least $950 billion on arms. If even 0.1 per cent of this was given to improve maternal mortality an unimaginable difference would be made. What could possibly prevent us from taking money which is used to kill people and instead using it to save them? I would also suggest that a team of trained medical staff would travel throughout the third world teaching villagers the basics on prenatal care, delivery, sanitation and the diagnosis of basic illnesses such as cervical and breast cancers and HIV/AIDS. Such knowledge should also be taught in schools throughout the world.

I urge you to support these goals and to fulfil your promise to the world. I urge you to do so not only because the fate of millions of people lies in your hands, but also because you want to. I urge you to fulfil your dream. I hope that someday I can go to sleep knowing that a healthy child has been born to a blissfully happy mother. I eagerly await the day when I can know that they will have a bright and wonderful future together. I hope that someday you shall be able to do the same and know that it was because of you. Thank you.

SHORTLIST – JUNIOR

Arun Murtagh

Aquinas Grammar School,
Belfast, Northern Ireland, Age 15

MDG 4 – REDUCE CHILD MORTALITY

Mr. President, Mr. Secretary-General, Ladies and Gentlemen, leaders of the free world, most of you gathered here today live a comfortable lifestyle. When you were young, you went to school and got an education. When you are hungry, you go to your fridge and get something to eat and when you are sick, you go to the doctor and receive medication. However, in our "free world" many are still chained to a life of poverty, still chained to a life of hunger, still chained to a life of disease, held down by the shackles of deprivation.

The aim of goal four is to reduce the rate of child mortality by two-thirds, but about 26,000 children under the age of five are dying every day, mainly from preventable causes, such as diarrhoea and pneumonia. Since I started this presentation, about ten children have died. This is unacceptable.

Let me tell you about the story of Parmesh. Parmesh was four years old. Just like any other child, he enjoyed his life, went to school where he learnt to read and write, played games with his siblings, as any other child would.

One day, Parmesh fell sick. Unfortunately, his parents could not afford to pay for a doctor. Parmesh died within the space of a day. Parmesh died of diarrhoea. Treatment for diarrhoea costs twenty pence. Twenty pence doesn't buy a lot today, but ladies and gentlemen, twenty pence could have saved Parmesh's life.

This story was covered by the *Guardian* in October of last year, nine years after the establishing of the Millennium Development Goals, and still preventable diseases are killing children, with only six years until the goal is due to be met.

In this country, diarrhoea is usually seen as a nuisance, but around 5,000 children each day are dying from diarrhoea. It is one of the biggest killers in the developing world. That very same infection that may cause you to miss a day of work or school is killing more children than aids, malaria and measles combined.

Think about the last time you've turned on a tap to get clean running water. Whether to get a drink, wash yourself or brush your teeth it's there on demand. Water is essential – 66 per cent of our body is made up of water, yet, in Africa, half of the population do not have access to clean, yet alone running, water. This is the main cause of diarrhoea. Something so simple that we take for granted everyday is killing hundreds of children every day. There needs to be change. We need solutions and the solutions are simple.

Projects such as rainwater harvesting, wells and pumps can help save people's lives, however money is needed to help save these people's lives. By providing clean water we could stop the spread of diarrhoea and other such harmful diseases; therefore, the UN urgently needs to fund projects for water for areas of deprivation.

The other part of the solution is healthcare. According to an article in the leading medical journal *The Lancet*, two-thirds of child deaths could be prevented if those children could get good-quality healthcare services.

There are many barriers to healthcare in the developing world. The main barrier is cost. In most developing countries, the poorest 20 per cent of the population has a child mortality rate that is two to four times higher than that of the wealthiest 20 per cent. Should the amount of money that one possesses really determine a life or death?

There are many costs for the poor trying to obtain healthcare, with user fees being the biggest barrier, however it is not the only barrier.

When you need to visit a doctor, you do not need to travel very far to reach one, maybe a couple of miles by car or bus? Imagine every time you are sick that you had to travel 20 kilometres on foot just to see a doctor. This also contributes to transport costs, which can cost up to fifty per cent of the total direct cost, effectively doubling the cost of the treatment.

The UN needs to fund projects to cut user fees, and provide localised, better quality healthcare services for all. If we can achieve the simple goal of cutting the preventable diseases, we can continue with the harder goals, one step at a time. This is not mission impossible; the resources are available.

The UN affirmed in the 2002 International Conference on Financing for Development, that "each of the developed countries would give 0.7 per cent of their gross national product (GNP) to Official Development Assistance". A goal of 0.7 per cent does not sound like a large figure, but to put that figure into perspective, 0.7 per cent of the USA's gross domestic product is just over $101 billion.

If each of the developed countries gave 0.7 per cent of their GNP by 2015, it would provide enough resources to meet the target. Unfortunately, this target is not on track. Most of the countries are not meeting the targets, such as the UK who had only gave over 0.4 per cent of their GNP as of 2008, and the USA, the world's richest country, had only given 0.18 per cent.

If the USA and UK can afford to give trillions to the banking sector, at their beck and call, surely they can afford $100 billion to people that need it most? Many may think that during a recession we must focus on other things but I urge you to continue your aid efforts. We cannot turn back. Spending on foreign aid is vital. Incompetence is not an option. This is our only chance.

And in years to come, we can say that we were the generation that pushed for a better tomorrow. We achieved the goals. We were the revolutionaries. We were the life changers.

As a great man once said: "Be the change you want to see in the world."

SHORTLIST – JUNIOR

Makinde Oluwadamilola

Loreto Secondary School,
Navan, Co. Meath, Ireland, Age 15

MDG 3 – PROMOTE GENDER EQUALITY AND EMPOWER WOMEN

Mr. President, Mr. Secretary-General, Ladies and Gentlemen, I would like to welcome you all to this year's United Nations General Assembly. It is both an honour and a privilege to be amongst you tonight and I would like to use this opportunity to thank you all for attending, reaffirming the commitment you have made on behalf of your respective countries to make this world a fairer, more equitable place for this generation and those to come.

In the year 2000, world leaders met in acknowledgment of the vast resources available to the privileged minority of the world and the bitter challenges faced by many others. Out of mutual understanding and respect, the Millennium Development Goals were born.

This document contained extraordinary statements that would shape the next 15 years in international aid relations, impressive yet wholly accessible. Great strides have been made towards the accomplishment of these goals, and yet there is still so much left to do, especially in the area of gender equality. As a female growing up in such a privileged society as Ireland, I am privy to the huge disparity in the treatment of women as opposed to that of men, due to my Nigerian origin. I can relate personal tales of intelligent female relations left to work the farm while boys of their age, in their families, attended school. The general attitude was "they're just girls anyway ... soon enough they'll get married and be gone".

I know many of you are probably wondering how this could be, but the stark reality is that this is still the mindset of many people around the world. While it is not possible to calculate the brain power lost due to this backward mentality, we can look to prevent your children and mine from ever being subjected to that level of blatant disregard. For me, to think of how different my life would be if my mum were a mere farm hand is beyond belief.

In West and Central Africa, the effect of drought and armed conflict on girls staying in school is more profound than on the boys, essentially because girls are the first to be withdrawn from school. As such, they require targeted intervention (such as promoting later marriage) which would help girls attend and stay in school. It is a very sad day for the world when we can say 75 per cent of the world's 876 million illiterate are women.

Those that are privileged to have undergone third-level education, as well as people like myself who are still in education, are well aware of the huge difference an education makes to your quality of life and your standard of living. Apart from the acquisition of skill, education gives an added sense of self-worth, something seldom felt by women who are constantly told they are life-long subjects to whatever oppressive system they belong to.

The legal discrimination of women in many countries undermines the position of women in society and continuously makes them easy targets for violence. Countries such as Lebanon, Saudi

Arabia and Egypt are governed by religion-based status codes, codes under which women are viewed as mere extensions of their male family members, be it fathers, husbands or brothers.

There is no way any women living under these conditions can be viewed as independent, which is a fundamentally flawed phenomenon. In many countries in the Middle-East/North Africa region, no specific laws exist to penalise domestic violence.

China's one child policy has heightened the disdain for female children; many are abandoned or left to die in preference for male children, while the Afghan government is keen on actively excluding girls from schooling. These are monumental obstacles, not only to gender equity, but also the run of diplomatic affairs. Women's rights need to be asserted now more than ever, and who better to do this than you, our leaders.

I am very conscious of the financial strains on each of your home economies, and how this could negatively influence your zeal in working towards the actualisation of these goals. Notwithstanding, one thing is clear – if women are put on the backbench till economic recovery begins, the situation would be much worse with needless losses incurred in the process. We need immediate, deliberate action and we need it now. We are investing in the futures of young girls around the world, we are liberating the women of today and we are doing what we can to ensure the well-being of *all* nations. In achieving this goal, you would have opened the door to the completion of the other seven.

In committing to the Millennium Development Goals, you have shown a true interest in the welfare of those you work for. You have shown the ability to discern when action is needed and what steps to take. This is an encouragement for all of you esteemed dignitaries to remember the reasons why you first committed to these goals, and a call for you to realise that those reasons are as valid now as they ever have been. In honouring your promises, you make it known throughout the world that you are leaders indeed, paving the way for much needed social reform.

My having received an education is the only thing that allows me stand before you today and articulate this huge burden felt by countless women. My having been given as equal voice as my male counterparts allowed this honour be bestowed on me. Your prompt and effective response to these pleas will one day allow me to hold my sons and daughters and say: "Because my leaders took a stand for justice, you will grow alongside each other with equal opportunities and an equal standing before all courts. Because of them your lives weren't ended before they began, because the leaders of yesterday upheld your right to a tomorrow, because of them!"

SHORTLIST – JUNIOR

Zoe Hayes

St Thomas Aquinas School,
Birmingham, England, Age 14

MDG 2 – ACHIEVE UNIVERSAL PRIMARY EDUCATION

Ten years ago, as I'm sure you don't need reminding, you set the goal to ensure that, by 2015, children everywhere, boys and girls alike, will be able to complete a full course of primary schooling and that therefore, in some respects, you do not need informing how important it is. However, I would like to remind you just why education is so important. It may horrify you that in Africa alone a child dies every three seconds, 45 people die from Aids a day. One in 16 women die from pregnancy or childbirth and that 771 million adults worldwide (64 per cent of whom are female) are illiterate.

When faced with the choice of all eight millennium goals to address today, achieving universal primary education seemed to be the ultimate solution to all. This is not just because I have a passion for education, or slate the British education system on a regular basis, which is perhaps a matter for another day, but because quite simply, none of the remaining seven goals could be achieved without this one. Frankly, we need to start combating problems from the core, and it would appear that ABC "would be a very good place to start".

Francis Bacon famously said that "knowledge is power". Power does not necessarily mean absolute control, but simply allows freedom and possibilities. Haiti is an epitome of this; the dominant language is Creole yet the legal language is French. Therefore, most people do not understand the law, providing them with no access to justice, which has resulted in serious oppression and poverty.

Julius Nyerere, the former President of the Republic of Tanzania, said that "education is not a way to escape poverty – it is a way of fighting it", and in saying this he was absolutely correct. An education helps people to build up industry; take the industrial revolution in Britain for example, once a primary education was compulsory and people could read and write, they understood health and safety rules allowing the death rate to fall dramatically. People also built up financially stable businesses which benefited both themselves and their country.

One of the most successful ways to eradicate or at least reduce poverty is to increase wealth, and I firmly believe that an education is the first step towards achieving this. We need to combine school education in less economically developed countries with the economic activities in the community. As an example, where fabric production, such as weaving, is dominant in the community, lessons based upon the fabric trade should be included in the curriculum, allowing an education to be truly useful and beneficial both to the individual, in a variety of different ways, and the economic development of the community. Additionally, schools would no longer be alienated from the society, but fully incorporated into it.

Combating HIV/AIDS is a millennium goal and figures suggest that HIV/AIDS infection rates double among young people who do not finish primary school and that if every girl and boy received a complete primary education, at least seven million new cases of HIV could be prevented in a decade. Therefore I can see no argument that an education would not hep to combat this issue too.

Moving on to gender equality, if two-thirds of children without an education are girls, how can we conceivably hope for gender equality? It is good old common sense that educated women have greater knowledge about health issues and greater bargaining power in the household, which has a positive impact on their own health and that of their children, and a figure deserving serious condemnation is that the failure to reach education targets by 2005 is estimated to have resulted in over one million unnecessary child and maternal deaths. This shows that education closely links to yet another millennium goal.

The UN Declaration on the Rights of the Child clearly states that every child has the right to a free education, but this is simply not enough. We need to be doing everything possible to educate the next generation, whoever and wherever they are. This may include providing transport to and from school, ensuring that *everything* related to the child's education is free or offering free meals and basic health services.

In many countries, school fees are a major barrier preventing children, particularly girls, from attending school. Seven million additional children entered school in Uganda, Tanzania, and Kenya alone when school fees were abolished.

Well-trained and supported teachers are also crucial for a good-quality education. However, there is currently a global shortage of two million teachers, and at least 15 million new teachers will be needed in the next five years in order to achieve education for all. This is a fact which I struggle to comprehend. What is the point in making promises if we fail to support them with actions?

For all of the preceding reasons, the achievement of this goal is crucial, however, 2015 is five years away and still in Sub-Saharan Africa, for example, around 38 million children of primary school age are still out of school, which is worsened by the fact that in Africa, once in school, there is only a one in three chance that a student will complete primary level.

It's all well and good having these ideals and aspirations but at the end of the day what is our problem? Are we really such control freaks that we can't or won't let people who we see as sufferers and victims help themselves and rise out of the flames? We have the plans in place, good on us, but the fact remains that 771 million adults in the world, that's about one in every six, are illiterate and many more than 72 million children in the developing world have no education. It really is appalling. Why are we so scared and insecure as to give people who have suffered a long history of hardship some choices or prospects of a future?

I would like to close with a parting thanks for your hospitality and attentiveness, but please remember that we are all here today because we can read and write. Just think what a girl from the developing world would want to say to you right now, and more importantly remember and act on the fact of why she quite simply couldn't.

SHORTLIST – JUNIOR

Ciara Moloney

Mean Scoil Mhuire, Longford, Ireland, Age 15

MDG 7 – ENSURE ENVIRONMENTAL SUSTAINABILITY

Mr. President, Mr. Secretary-General, Ladies and Gentlemen,

Tick, tock. Tick, tock. Tick, tock. Ten years down, five to go.

When first published, the Millennium Development Goals were put forward as our saviours. Eight goals, signed up to by all 192 UN member states, as well as at least 23 international organisations. They used big, utopian words like "universal" and "equality" and "global partnership". But we believed in the goals – and we believed that we could achieve them by 2015, because 2015 seemed an awfully long way away.

Today, I want to talk about goal seven. If the MDGs were a litter, goal seven would most definitely be the runt. "To ensure environmental sustainability," it reads. Next to world hunger and gender equality, it sounds like small potatoes.

Allow me to clear this matter up. Environmental sustainability is anything but small potatoes. Environmental sustainability is the biggest potatoes you have ever encountered.

Goal seven divides into four basic targets: introducing sustainable development and reversing the loss of environmental resources; reducing biodiversity loss; halving the proportion of people without access to safe drinking water and basic sanitation; and finally, improving the lives of at least 100 million slum dwellers.

Let's start with target 7A: "Integrate the principles of sustainable development into country policies and programmes and reverse the loss of environmental resources." It's a bit of a tongue twister, I'll grant you that, but a simple enough ideal. We need to combat climate change. According to a report by the Pew Research Centre, only 36 per cent of Americans believe in man-made climate change. Presumably, the other 64 per cent disagree with this particular target.

The scariest thing about these figures is that it is precisely these people who have caused the climate catastrophe, but it is the people of the developing world who will suffer.

Tick, tock.

Target 7B comes next: "Reduce biodiversity loss, achieving, by 2010, a significant reduction in the rate of loss." Some things specifically mentioned here include fish, forests and protected areas.

Currently, only 22 per cent of the world's fisheries are sustainable. 35 years ago, this figure was 40 per cent. Clearly the MDGs have failed to improve the fish situation. Next up, forests. Between 2000 and 2005, there has been a net decline in forest area of about 7.3 million hectares. The deforestation rate has been fastest in hugely bio-diverse areas, including Latin America and Oceanica. Another failure on target 7B.

Protecting of terrestrial and marine area. Only 0.7 per cent of the world's oceans were put under protection.

Tick, tock.

Target 7C naturally follows, and I'm afraid we're in for more of the same. "Halve the proportion of people without sustainable access to safe drinking water and basic sanitation." One billion people do not have access to safe drinking water. That means one in six people do not have the access to that most basic of human needs. Two and a half billion don't have access to basic sanitation. This isn't some thing you can just explain away – one in six people do not have access to safe drinking water, *one in six*.

Tick, tock.

And now, ladies and gentlemen, we come to our final target: to have achieved a significant improvement in the lives of at least

100 million slum dwellers. That is 10 per cent of slum dwellers. Even if you manage to achieve this, 90 per cent of slum dwellers will still lead the same lives. Lives full of hardship that you cannot even imagine. I want to live in a world where no one leads such lives; where there is decent, affordable housing for the poor. That is a basic human right – the UN, of all organisations, surely understands basic human rights?

Tick, tock.

Ladies and gentlemen, I am not saying progress has not been made. It has. Yet the idea persists that environmental sustainability is the runt of the pack. It persists that it is merely small potatoes. Goal seven is a mission to change this.

Ten years down, five to go.

Tick, tock. Tick, tock. Tick, tock.

SHORTLIST – JUNIOR

Eibhlin Lonergan

Loreto Secondary School, Fermoy,
Co. Cork, Ireland, Age 15

MDG 1 – ERADICATE EXTREME POVERTY AND HUNGER

Mr. Secretary-General, Ladies and Gentlemen,

I feel greatly honoured and humbled to receive an invitation from the Secretary-General of the United Nations to address such a distinguished gathering of world leaders. The subject of my talk is the first of the eight Millennium Development Goals which you drew up, and signed, back in the year 2000, and for which you set a target date of 2015. This first goal is "to eradicate extreme poverty and hunger." Of the eight highly commendable and praiseworthy goals which you laid down as your prime agenda for the coming fifteen years, I consider this to be the most urgent and necessary, as all the other goals, more or less, depend on the achievement of this goal.

In the last ten years some earth-shattering disasters, both natural and political, have occurred throughout the world. Your efforts, as world leaders, to alleviate the sufferings of the pitiful conditions of these disaster-stricken areas are worthy of the highest praise. The heart-rending scenes from Haiti and Chile, the tsunami-devastated citizens of Eastern Asia and the famine stricken countries of Africa all prompt response from your governments. But it is now timely, and essential, to take stock of the efforts of the past ten years in attaining your goals, and to lay out a strategy for the next five years. As Gro Harlem Brundtland so eloquently put it: "The library of life is burning, and we don't even know the titles of the books."

Here are a few sobering thoughts. One in six people in our world today does not have enough to eat. Every year throughout the world almost ten million children die before their fifth birthday. The World Bank estimates that child deaths in Africa alone could grow by an additional 700,000 per year. The problem is not that there is a lack of food. The real problem is the lack of access to food and the lack of willingness of the developed world to share the produce of the earth with their starving brothers in the underdeveloped countries. Over the past twenty-five years global food production has grown more rapidly than global population. Yet there are millions of children starving. Fr. Bertrand Aridtide uses a very appropriate metaphor to describe this unbalanced situation: "The world is like a table. Twenty per cent live on the table and eighty per cent live underneath it... Our task is to move the table, to change its position if necessary, and all to sit together around the table."

The Chinese have an old proverb that says if we give a man a fish, he has food for a day, but if we teach him to fish he has food for a lifetime. Financial relief is laudable in time of crises, but, in the long term, more than this alone is required. We must remember that very often these deprived people have no access to land, water, markets, credit or expertise. While voluntary organisations, such as Goal or Concern from my own country, Ireland, have done Trojan work in organising self-help projects, their efforts are limited. An international input from all your governments is obviously called for. Here the funds can be properly supervised, the expertise of engineers, economists and technicians can be supplied, the necessary technology and machinery made available and, most importantly, the necessary education and training for the native population supplied. I am certain that within a limited period, the lives of thousands of men, women and children will be transformed. As these people take control of their own destiny, their pride and self-confidence will grow, when they no longer will depend on the "crumbs that fall from the rich man's table".

I urge you, as world leaders, to just contemplate what hunger and poverty means in the underdeveloped countries. Just pause in your busy day and see in your mind's eye the emaciated little bodies of some starving children. There they lay impassively with their protruding bones, their bloated stomachs, their wrinkled little faces which would seem more in place on some octogenarian. Their eyes have lost the zest for life, which a mere bowl of rice per day might restore. There, quietly keeping watch over her starving family sits an equally emaciated mother, whose years of sacrifice, endeavouring to keep the life in her children, have finally broken her health and spirit. Compare this image to what we in the developed world call hunger and poverty. If children had to miss one meal during the day, or if their parents could not afford a visit to McDonald's, we would begin to talk about deprivation and poverty. Perhaps this type of image should help us to get our priorities right, and might influence us in making a choice between the purchase of arms, or the funding of space travel and putting the essentials for life in the mouths of the starving masses. We all realise that we are in the middle of a recession. However, I would urge you to succumb to the temptation to cut back on foreign aid to the hungry and deprived of the world. After all, the man with no shoes thought he was badly off until he met a man with no legs.

I thank sincerely Mr. Ban Ki Moon, Secretary General of the United Nations, for affording me the opportunity to express my views to such a distinguished and influential audience as you, the world leaders. My deep gratitude goes to you for giving me so much of your valuable time, and paying such close attention to my humble opinion. As no less a person than Barack Obama, President of the United States, put it so succinctly: "Change will not come if we wait for some other person or some other time. We are the ones we've been waiting for. We are the change that we seek." Let us then look forward to 2015, with another exhortation from President Obama as our catch-cry: "Yes we can!"

SHORTLIST – JUNIOR

Matthew Salit

*Dr Kevin M. Hurley Middle School,
Seekonk, Massachusetts, USA, Age 15*

MDG 1 – ERADICATE EXTREME POVERTY AND HUNGER

Mr. President, Mr. Secretary-General, Ladies and Gentlemen,

Hello. Marhaba. Ni Hao. Bonjour. Hola. Konnichiwa. We have come together as a whole today to work toward a common goal, though we are all different in many ways. We are different in our customs, languages, successes, and failures. We have different opinions, different histories, and different conflicts. For an outsider looking in, this meeting is no more than a cluster of nations with outlandish and nearly ridiculous goals.

But goals we have. These goals, eight in number, have brought us together. The goals, on their own, are simply fantasies; irresolvable challenges. But together, goals combined with countries united, will save the world from its own greatest creature; humans.

Like a checklist, we must begin with our most urgent and essential drawback, world hunger. World hunger is the want or scarcity of food in a country, and it is no wonder why it is literally goal #1. This devastating issue, combined with treatable diseases, takes the lives of more than 10 million children every year. This is the equivalent of more than 30,000 deaths per day, or one every three seconds. At any given moment, there are nearly one billion people suffering from starvation. That is about one in every seven persons, or 14 per cent of the world population.

Yes, eight goals we have, but solving one could solve the rest. Nearly every single one of our goals is directly related to world hunger and poverty. One of our goals includes universal education. This goal is directly linked to impoverished nations, the same nations influenced by world hunger. These countries are also the most heavily affected by gender inequality, poor child heath, and poor maternal health. Developing nations should be, and are, the primary target for assistance.

One specific example of world hunger directly related to another problem is Ndifor Eleves Funnui's story. He is from the impoverished nation of Niger, and he says, in a letter to Barak Obama: "Sir, know that because of hunger, children leave school and end up on the streets where they become vulnerable and are manipulated. Girls become prostitutes, and live dangerously as they try to survive. They are many girls that have sex in exchange for food. We all know the relationship between unprotected sex and HIV/AIDS. When these children are hungry and vulnerable, terrorist groups easily manipulate and send them on suicide missions. This is why I am asking you to first of all fight hunger if you want to fight HIV/AIDS and terrorism."

World hunger is upon us for many reasons, some of which we truly cannot control. These include famines, droughts, and other natural disasters. However, many of the actions that are linked to world hunger are our own fault. As with anything else, money is a (if not the) primary cause of starvation.

Debt repayments take away from many of the funds for hunger and disaster relief. Before the recent earthquake that struck this once enslaved nation, Haiti was in debt about $641 million. This does not sound like very much, especially compared to the United States' $12.6 trillion and counting debt, but the annual wage per Haitian is only about $730. With only $7.3 billion in the country overall, there is very little money going towards the debt. Now, 200,000 people are dead, there is $7.8 billion of damage, and the western hemisphere's least developed nation is taking steps backwards.

Armed conflict also influences world hunger economically and physically. Military forces and organized crime can destroy crops, food stocks, live stocks, homes, and farms. In addition, it is estimated that just $30 billion every year would account for ending world hunger. The Borgen Project puts this into perspective. $170 billion is spent annually for the US war, while an additional $230 billion is paid to US military contractors every year. Many in my country (the United States) are furious with the fact that soldiers are still in the Middle East at this very moment. If we bring home enough troops for just 13 per cent of the wage of military contractors, we will have the $30 billion needed to annually end starvation and malnourishment.

Poverty and hunger are often mistaken as just affecting Africa. This is certainly not true. Nearly every country in the world has portions that are impoverished or starving. On average, 32.6 per cent of citizens of a country are below the poverty line. However, 15 of the 17 most impoverished nations are African. There are many reasons for starvation in Africa, some which we can easily change; others we cannot. Some causes I have stated earlier, but one not mentioned is government turmoil. Since 1980, there have been at least 32 successful coups d'état in Africa, all of which resulted in major political and economical changes. These successful military takeovers are among countless failed attempts. Each leading group brings with them different ideas, many of which contradict the plans of the system they took over. Every change seems to hurt the economy, as the facts support this statement. There is no perfect government system, but a stable one is a successful one.

The world is full of thinkers, and that is great. Thinkers came up with this list, and thinkers brought us here together today. But thinkers are only good for thinking. The world needs doers, as doers are the ones who can bring about change. Doers are the ones who are going to get the $300 billion in the next five years to reach the Millennium Goals by 2015. Doers accomplish things, and a doer I am.

Thank you for your time and I look forward to an Age of Doers who move us towards accomplishing our eight goals soon.

SHORTLIST – JUNIOR

Hannah Heeran

Dominican College, Wicklow, Ireland, Age 13

MDG 2 – ACHIEVE UNIVERSAL PRIMARY EDUCATION

Mr. President, Mr. Secretary-General, Ladies and Gentlemen,

As a child in a developed country, I have all that I need. I have a place to sleep that is sheltered from rain and the cold, I have food and water, I have the privilege of being able to attend school until college, I have a lot of the things I want but do not necessarily need. For me life is easy, for a child in a third world country it is not.

I am writing to you to raise your awareness and ask your help to achieve universal primary education. Education is so important in the world as without out it children and adults are not able to build the foundations needed to create a stable life for themselves and their families. When the children are needed at home to get water or food, they are deprived of education, ensuring that they will not have the life they deserve when they grow older. It's a vicious circle, and the only way to break it is to help us provide basic primary education for people in third world countries.

Education is a human right and has been recognised as such since the 1948 adoption of the Universal Declaration on Human rights. Since then numerous human rights treaties have reaffirmed this right and have supported the entitlement to free, compulsory education for all the children of the world, particularly girls, those in difficult circumstances, or those of ethnic minorities. Based on enrolment data, about 72 million children of a primary age in the developing world were without an education in 2005; 57 per cent of these were girls and this was considered to be an optimistic number.

Although it may seem like an expensive undertaking, the fact it that if we had spent less than one per cent of what the world spends on weaponry we could have put every child in school by the year 2000 and yet it didn't happen. This just shows you that if we achieved world peace, then we could achieve universal primary education easily. "Which is more important, winning a feud, or conquering the problem of global education?"

Although convincing the important governments of the world to help with achieving this issue is important, appealing to us, the general public, can make a huge difference. If all of us could just be aware of what's going on in the world around us, and be reminded that while we may think our lives are hard and while we wake up in the morning complaining about school, that there are young children out there who would love to have the opportunity to go to school, but don't due to their family circumstances, the country in which they live and other factors that prevent them from achieving an education they have a right to. "Should anyone be deprived of their rights?"

Let me tell you the story of Huan Qing Hua. At age 14, Huan and her little sister, Huan Qing Mei, were found sitting side by side in Tang Lian. Like most of their peers the girls spent their days cooking for the family, doing the laundry and carrying water. These are not unusual aspects of rural life where they come from. Ask a little girl in Na Ma, Chong Tao or any rural area "what do you do for fun?" and the answer may often sadly be "sweep the floor". Now ask yourself, is this what you consider fun? What do you consider to be a good way to pass the time? Is this what these girls should be replying? Fun feels like an extravagant concept when you see that villages survive on weather conditions, surviving health mishaps and harvesting good crops.

Children in these places, in their spare time, work! These two girls have three other sisters; their mother left them five years ago out of shame for having all girls Should a mother be really so ashamed of having girls that she would abandon them? Children like these are children without a childhood and education. Girls like Huan Qing Hua may not have the language to express their dreams or dreams to express, but they are unequivocally aware of the pain that is theirs.

So you see, girls like Huan Qing and her sisters need an education to survive and have a chance at life. To experience things that in our world we designate as fun. Let me ask you a question which everyone should ask themselves when thinking of the millions of people without an education to start them off in life. "How would you feel if your children had a life like this, if your nieces or nephews had to experience the burden of keeping a family alive, if your siblings were deprived of their childhood to work, just to earn money to scrape enough food together for their loved ones to persevere in life? How would you feel if this was you?"

Around 121 million children are without education worldwide right now. One of the very sad things is that as we are nearing our deadline, 2015, progress in education has actually slowed during the year 2010. Shouldn't it be the other way around? If we manage to overcome the astounding global problem of children without a primary education, the world would be a better place, a place more educated, a world where every person had the opportunity to dream their dreams, and most importantly, for once in their life give them the hope that they can someday achieve their dreams. Knocking down this hurdle that confines people to their way of living, we, as a global community, can make earth a better place for our children, grandchildren and those to be in years to come.

I hope you can see why achieving universal primary education is an extremely important issue in the world and that if accomplished will build the foundations we need to eliminate other world issues such as hunger and poverty. So I say, *"Now,* not to-morrow or next year, but *now* is the time to take action and really achieve what we have been slowly anticipating."

Shortlist – Junior

Emma McLaughlin
Coláiste Idé, An Daingean Ui Chúis,
Co. Kerry, Ireland, Age 15

MDG 4 – Reduce Child Mortality

Mr. President, Mr. Secretary-General, Ladies and Gentlemen,

By the end of this speech, 80 children under the age of five in the developing world will have lost their lives.

Ladies and gentlemen, I want to remind you of a meeting that took place as we entered the new millennium, one that was full of enthusiasm, excitement, motivation and resolution. Eight promises called the Millennium Development Goals were made by world leaders to the developing world. Ladies and Gentlemen, I urge you to connect with the past to save the future and reach back to that day; to the feeling of possibility and the sense of a new beginning, to listen to the pleas of the world and to achieve those goals, because not only did you make promises to the developing world, but to the entire world. That day was a decade ago, and right now there are exactly 1,710 days left until 2015 arrives.

Under-five child mortality is one devastating horror that faces us today. At that famous meeting, you promised to reduce child mortality. In my opinion, it is one of the most worthy goals, as everybody has the right to life. There is a brick wall of statistics and mortality rates being built by poverty at the moment. It is a tragic fact that millions die each year under the age of five from preventable causes. If these rates continue as they are, then by the year 2015, around 50 million more children under the age of five will have died unnecessarily. We need to listen; listen to the pleas of the poor, to the cries of the children and to the words of others.

"Children are the future", but so many have no future.

The facts are frightening: millions die each year. Half of child deaths occur in Africa. In 2006, out of every 1,000 births in industrialised countries, an average of six died under the age of five, in developing countries the average was 79. A child in Sierra Leone, the country with the world's highest under-five mortality rate – 262 out of 1,000 births in 2007 – is 87 times more likely to die than a Swedish child (rate of three out of 1,000 births). One in six children in Sub-Saharan Africa dies before their fifth birthday. Ultimately, every six seconds, another child has lost their lives before the age of five.

Whatever about numbers, facts and figures, though, it is our moral duty to help these children, these families, these countries. Each of those dead children was somebody's daughter, son, sister, brother or best friend. Now they are just a nameless number. Nobody wants to admit this or treat the dead with disrespect, but such is the scale of the problem at this point.

Ladies and gentlemen, I'm sure most of you have children, nieces or nephews. Think about them for a moment. Remember the last time you brought them to the playground or a birthday party. Think about watching them play make-believe, and wondering at their wonder. Now think about Third World children, their backs bent with poverty. Their playground might be a decaying log, any party they had would be dry and they make-believe that someday they will not feel hunger. But for millions their dreams do not come true – they die before they have lived.

Listen to the words of others. John Donne said, "No man is an island," but how many of you know what comes next? It is this:

"No man is an island. Every man is a continent – a piece of the main. Every man's death diminishes me, for I am involved in mankind."

He had the right idea, as you can see.

So what does it come down to? I am sure that all of you know that the five main causes of child mortality are malaria, measles, malnutrition, diarrhoea and acute respiratory illness. In developed countries, children receive vaccinations for measles, malnutrition is more or less unheard of, asthma is the most common respiratory illness and that was sorted long ago with medicines and inhalers, diarrhoea does not affect us badly, due to our nutritious fibre-filled diets and if your child got a mosquito bite, there would be a selection of creams waiting for you to buy in the local pharmacy.

Can you see, ladies and gentlemen, how severe the inequality is, and how it is killing the under-privileged children of this world? Their systems are weakened by hunger and disease is crippling their bodies. Lack of food and a nutritious diet hinders the effectiveness of medicines for those who are lucky enough to have access to them. And that is not all, since the HIV/AIDS pandemic began, 25 million people have died, causing more than 15 million children to lose at least one parent.

These children are in desperate need of our help; poverty and hunger are beating them and disease is devastating them. This is a goal worthy of our generation. We need to wake up and take heed.

Listen to the words of others: Eavan Boland wrote in her poem "Child of Our Time" of a dead child that she wished to:

> *"Find for your sake whose life our idle*
> *Talk has cost, a new language, Child*
> *Of our time, our times have robbed your cradle."*

We do need to find a new language – one where the words "poverty", "hunger", "failure", "disease" and "inequality" do not exist.

We need to end this idle talk of promises and act on it. We must sing a new language of hope out to these betrayed children – but it is more than hope, it is a 100 per cent possibility.

So what can we actually do? Well, most children could be saved by low-tech, evidence-based cost-effective measures. Simple things that are taken for granted by us in industrialised countries – vaccines, antibiotics, nutrient supplementations. For those to work, hunger must be eradicated. Food schemes can be set up whereby villages are given animals to farm, therefore producing their own food products and perhaps availing of transport as well. This is already happening due to the fantastic work of voluntary charities such as Trócaire and Concern, but we need more. Helping people help themselves is the first step on the path out of poverty.

Children are dying of malaria. So why doesn't every child have the most obvious preventative – insecticide-treated bed-nets? They come at pennies apiece.

Improved family care is necessary – education should be provided to mothers on how to make simple changes to living conditions, e.g. improving hygiene and sanitation, therefore improving the health of the child. This is connected to gender inequality – women simply do not have enough knowledge. If maternal health is improved then it stands to reason that the health of the children will be improved. Breastfeeding practices should be set up – as it is an excellent way to ensure infant health, especially up to the age of six months.

Fresh water that is safe to drink would do absolute wonders. Africa has been drained dry by drought. The people are dehydrated and dying of thirst. Water is vital to us all. Sanitation and hygiene are two more massive problems in the fight against child mortality. I wonder how many of you have ever thought of washing your hands as a luxury? Wells must be built, and lots of them.

Improved education would make way for doctors and less disease. We must educate the people themselves so that they can become self-sufficient and help themselves and each other.

To help the children, we must help the communities, the tribes, the families – because this is a family affair. That is why it is such a sensitive topic – almost everybody has loved a child: a brother or sister, a cousin, a best friend, a daughter or a son. We read in magazines and newspapers about tragic stories of children who have lost their lives, but we seem to accept that this travesty "just happens" in the developing world. How many of those African children do you think will be laid to rest in peace in a little white coffin?

We need to examine ourselves. Who are we? What are our values? Do we value life, equality, health, happiness? Listen to the words of others: Bono said:

> *"It is, or it ought to be unacceptable that an accident of longitude and latitude determines whether a child lives or dies. Beyond our own borders we have offered excuses instead of solutions."*

Excuses are no longer an option, indifference is no longer an option and another broken promise is simply no longer an option. Act of participation is the only solution. So, ladies and gentlemen, enough dawdling, we need to start sprinting because the finish line is only 1,710 days away. Momentum is building but disease is still way ahead. When we reach that new dawn of 2015, the sun will not be killing the crops of the Third World, or cracking their skin and scratching their throats, but it will be shining gloriously down on them and greeting them for a new morning, a new beginning. This is the dream of our generation, but we have a right to be dreamers.

I thank you very much for your time, ladies and gentlemen, but before I finish I would like to ask you one last time to listen to the words of others. John Lennon's famous song "Imagine" has touched the hearts of millions for a reason.

"Imagine there's no countries,
I wonder if you can,
Nothing to live or die for,
A brotherhood of man.
Imagine all the people
Living for today.
You may say I'm a dreamer,
But I'm not the only one.
I hope someday you'll join me,
And the world can live as one."

One. Wouldn't it be nice…?

PASSAGES/EXTRACTS/QUOTES
– JUNIOR CATEGORY

Mark McDermott

St. Columba's College, Lifford,
Co. Donegal, Ireland, Age 14

MDG 1 – ERADICATE EXTREME POVERTY AND HUNGER

… As you can see, the problems of world poverty and hunger are so closely linked that they can be described as one problem. The problem is focused in the same areas and regions. The problem is focused in the poorest areas of the world called the Third World. If even a small fraction of the poor people living in poverty and hunger were living in a First World country, such as the USA, Britain, Germany or France, world poverty and hunger would be a major political issue. Governments would be rushing to do something before the general public demand them to leave office. Yet here in the United Nations, where world nations stand together as a united world, not divided into First, Second and Third Worlds, we have a medium for solving the problem, yet the problem is not being given the attention it is due.

However, the United Nations has committed itself to these problems before. I would love to tell you had solved them, but you have not solved them at all. You set eight Millennium Development Goals 10 years ago, and the first one was "Halve between 1990 and 2015, the proportion of people whose income is less than one dollar a day", and "Halve, between 1990 and 2015, the proportion of people who suffer from hunger". In parts of Asia, Latin

America, the Caribbean and especially in Sub-Saharan Africa these goals are not being reached. To the 1.2 billion in poverty, and to the 815 million in hunger, the Millennium Development Goals have meant nothing! It is only five years and counting until 2015. Two thirds of the time is up. You need to do something, because the 1.2 billion in poverty and the 815 million hungry are silently crying out for help. Their plea is being ignored. Despite the economic difficulties, there is still money available to you. I am asking you to invest this money in meeting the Millennium Development Goals. You know what great work charities are trying to do on the ground, providing food, setting up agricultural projects such as irrigation schemes. They are making a difference, but they need your help to solve this problem. Today I appeal to you to work together, reach out to the workers on the ground and solve this problem. The problem of world poverty and hunger is a far bigger and more important problem than the economic crisis! If you could make a difference, it could define a generation. When you retire from office, you would be able to say, "I tried hard, I made a difference, I am proud". Do not end up saying, "I was involved in setting targets, but unfortunately they were not met". That would be meaningless.

So I set us all a challenge. Take action. Reset the first Millennium Development Goal to halve world poverty and hunger. Make sure the promise is kept, and do not stop trying until the goal is met. Remember, we have just five years and counting!

Sophie Poll

Bournemouth Collegiate School, Dorset,
United Kingdom, Age 14

MDG 2 – ACHIEVE UNIVERSAL PRIMARY EDUCATION

I am 14 years old and I am writing to you to show you that I strongly believe that every person on this planet deserves an education.

> *"Education is not the answer to the question. Education is the means to the answer to all questions."* -- William Allin

If this is true, then 30 per cent of the world will never know the answer. If we let them have the information, then we can give them the tools to answer the question. Only last year, over £1,500 was spent on a duck house. Imagine how many people could have been saved. £6,648 was spent on a garden. That could have helped 906 people get an education, but instead they carried on not knowing the answer.

We live a modern life, with electric toothbrushes, kettles, televisions, game players, music players and computers. If we changed these things for money, and gave the money to Less Economically Developed Countries, then they can receive an education and become the next Armstrong, Thatcher and Einstein.

When we give children the right to acquire knowledge, they then have control of their future, their health and the generations to come. Becoming educated means they can then become educators and ensure that future generations to come will continue to grow and cultivate their countries. For instance, they could develop their own health system, their own law system and their own sanitary system. With the new health and sanitary systems, their life expectancy is ensured to be longer. Using this, not only can they become teachers themselves but they can also help preserve their own cultures, religions and traditions. They can write down the rules and the celebrations that are important to their way of life. A more educated generation can then help the country be more independent and stop relying on other countries for support and their survival.

Are we taking advantage of those with less opportunity? Are we turning a blind eye on what we know is wrong? We are using the less fortuned and the poorer countries to subsidise our way of life by buying products from manufacturers that use cheap labour. It gets worse. In many poorer countries, there is no such thing as compulsive education. It is the children who are often the ones being employed for cheap labour. If these children were provided with an education, then they would not be working long hours, they would be learning. Your children go to school every day without thinking twice. In those countries, a lot of children from the age of five go to work every day without thinking twice.

In African countries, children as young as ten are being called into the army; they will not have a childhood. They will not have the wonderful childhood memories that so many of us remember. Their memories will be of fighting, running and shooting. But worst of all, they will have the memories of killing people; the memories of hearing the screams of dying men. Do we want this to be the way children remember the world? If we let these children have an education, then they can choose to fight in the army. They can choose to go to university, instead of being forced to kill people. Education gives people the chance to choose their future, instead of the government deciding it for them. If the children have an education, they can go to the army, not out of force, but out of choice. Imagine how they must feel now, wanting to go home. Then imagine how they will feel if they choose for themselves. Then they will feel proud to defend their country.

"Education costs money, but then so does ignorance."–
Sir Claus Moser

We can stop letting ignorance cost by not letting education cost. Education is not only a tool but a necessity. If we give children the tools, then they can decide their future and help others to decide their future. I am 14 years old and I strongly believe that achieving Universal Primary Education could have an enormous effect on starvation, poverty and our future world.

Ciara Kelleher

Salesian College, Limerick, Ireland, Age 14

MDG 1 – ERADICATE EXTREME POVERTY AND HUNGER

… As Bono once said: "If you want to eliminate hunger, everyone has to be involved." Now in order to meet our targets, we have to be at least halfway through reducing by half the proportion of people living on less than a dollar a day. We are a long way away from reducing by half the proportion of people suffering from hunger because as I said, 30,000 children a day die from hunger. Increasing the number of cents is increasing a little food, and maybe is increasing the life expectancy but not the standard of living. People are still undernourished and hungry.

Think about your own families at home, your children, your brothers and sisters. It is easy to sit and do nothing when your families are healthy and well fed. This project will take time and in the words of Jesse Owens: "We all have dreams, but in order to make dreams come into reality, it takes an awful lot of determination, dedication, self-discipline and effort." Or in Mother Teresa's words: "If you can't feed a hundred people then just feed one." Every person can make a difference.

It is a person's right to have certain things, for example, the Universal Declaration of Rights, Article 25 states that: "Everyone has the right to a standard of living adequate for the health and well-being of himself and his family." This includes food, clothing, housing, medical care and the right to security if sick, widowed or other lack of livelihood in circumstances beyond his control. I urge you to try harder and to make our goals a reality because every little helps.

> *"When a poor person dies it has not happened because God did not take care of him or her, it has happened because neither you nor I wanted to give that person what they needed"* – Mother Teresa

I once read that Joseph Stalin said: "The death of one man is a tragedy, the death of millions is a statistic." Unfortunately, that is the horrible truth. If you lose a parent it is a horrible time and grieving can take years. In Brazil families are dying in their millions and we have it in our power to change that and sometimes nobody does anything because it seems so far away from what we know or are accustomed to.

Together we can stop this.

What would you do if it was your family?

Rosin Lonergan

Our Lady's Grammar School, Newry,
Northern Ireland, Age 14

MDG 1 – ERADICATE EXTREME POVERTY AND HUNGER

Good morning. Mr President, Mr Secretary-General, Delegates, Ladies and Gentlemen. It is my honour to address you today on behalf of the children of the world.

I wrote this speech on my laptop in my bedroom, just after having eaten my dinner with my family. When I finished I listened to my Ipod for an hour while drinking coke and eating biscuits, then I watched television until 10.30 and I later went to bed. It was a very normal day and I didn't consider it special in any way. The reason for this is that I take all these things for granted. All my friends do the same ...

How lucky are we?

However, while I was writing this speech, somewhere in the world, over 25,000 children died from hunger, thirst and easily preventable diseases. Eighteen children died since I began talking. Ten years ago the United Nations created a committee to deal with and find a solution to the problem of poverty and starvation in the world. Regardless of what has been done so far ... Is it enough?

Last year governments of the world spent $1.5 trillion on military equipment. This includes warships, fighter planes, advanced satellite systems to detect missile launches and money to pay soldiers in war zones. Although countries must have armies and must be able to defend themselves against attack, this is a huge amount of money to spend annually in so-called "peacetime".

A tiny fraction of the amount spent could end poverty and starvation throughout the world forever. Systems could be put in place to ensure Third World countries could become self-sufficient with resources to provide future sustainability.

In my opinion, as a 14 year old girl, it appears that someone has got their priorities wrong.

Annually the EU has at least 15 million tonnes of food stored in huge warehouses throughout Europe. This is food which was grown by farmers but because there was too much of it, some had to be stored and most of that will end up getting dumped. This doesn't make sense to me.

I am not here to talk to you about global partnership, however greater communication between countries could without a doubt help solve world hunger and poverty. If all countries had the same laws and were all in agreement they could reach a solution to solve poverty and starvation. I believe that better communication between governments and controls on the amount of produce would save millions of pounds and this money or the excess food could be given to charities such as Concern.

Megan Carey

Loreto Secondary School, Fermoy,
Co. Cork, Ireland, Age 15

MDG 7 – ENSURE ENVIRONMENTAL SUSTAINABILITY

... I am 15 years old. Should I live life with the fear of what will happen tomorrow, or should I make sure that the world will still be here tomorrow and the next day for my children and my grandchildren and many generations to come? As one in six billion I can make a small difference – but in order to make a big difference I need your help.

I don't have a revolutionary solution that will ensure environmental sustainability. I wish I could show you a device that will fix the holes in the ozone layer or filter car emissions of all carbon dioxide. But I have to tell you that neither can you. My mother always says, "if you can't fix it, then don't break it". We can't fix what we have already broken. We can't put trees where there was once a magnificent forest that is now a desert – and we can't bring back animals and plants that have gone extinct, but what we can do is stop breaking what we still have. We can stop cutting down forests that are still there. We can stop the polar bears and pandas and other animals and plants from going extinct and we can stop the holes in the ozone growing more serious.

As far as I remember it was an adult who told me to share my toys and it was an adult who told me not to call people names. It was an adult who told me to be nice to others and to work with other people when I would like to do something that can't be done on my own. So why can't you practice what you preach? Lead us children by example save the world while you can.

I believe that we can achieve environmental sustainability if we work towards it and work together – adults and children alike. We can work together to achieve environmental sustainability. It starts right here, right now – my future and the future of the children of the world lies in your hands. The world will follow you if you show us that you are serious about achieving this goal. I want to be able to show my children all the beautiful things in the world before they are gone. I know this is one of the last goals that you will tackle but I assure you, I know that small changes make a big difference. If you agree to earnestly begin right now then please let your actions reflect your words.

Orla O'Gorman

Laurel Hill Colaiste, Limerick,
Ireland, Age 13

MDG 4 – REDUCE CHILD MORTALITY

There are only five years left so we need to get a move on. At the rate we are at now 53 of 60 priority countries will not succeed in achieving the goal unless we shake a leg. In my opinion there are five things we need to do to achieve our goal.

Number 1 – We need to make clean water available to every child in the developing world. This could be done by volunteers creating wells and water pumps in developing countries. I know that Concern and Trocaire do a lot of projects like this, but I think it should be done a lot more. Volunteers who work with these agencies should teach those in the developing world how to create wells and water pumps. This would enable more clean water to be available nearer to home, for all the children in developing countries. As a result, the creation of clean water sources nearer to children's homes would mean that more children could attend school as they would not be spending their day fetching dirty water from rivers.

Number 2 – We need to ensure that every child in the developing world has access to medical care. This would save the lives of many children who die from preventable diseases every day. This could be done by educating a person in each village on how to treat the most common diseases. They could then start up clinics and hospitals funded by charities and developed countries, which would result in a lot less deaths in the developing world. These clinics and hospitals need to be equipped with medical supplies; I think that charity organisations should set up a global gift initiative, which would fund medical supplies for these hospitals and clinics.

Number 3 – We need to get factories and industries into the developing countries. I would see a great benefit in large multinational companies investing in these countries. This would result in the creation of much needed employment.

Number 4 – We need to make sure every child in the developing world gets at least a primary education. This would mean that children of educated parents in the developing world would be twice as likely to live over the age of five. This could be done by charities setting up schools. I know this is already an ongoing project for charity organisations but more must be done in this area.

Number 5 – We need to help people in the developing world help themselves. Not only should volunteers be going over to developing countries but they should be teaching those in the developing world how to be teachers and how to be doctors. This would create employment, education, medical personnel and a lot more.

As you can see, there is much to be done if we want to achieve our goal in five years' time. Every single person in this world has a role to play if we want this to work.

Alyah Ali

Challney High School for Girls, Luton,
United Kingdom, Age 15

MDG 1- ERADICATE EXTREME POVERTY AND HUNGER

Mr. President, Mr. Secretary-General, Ladies and Gentlemen,

You have asked me to speak, for which I am grateful, for had you not done so, I would have spoken out nonetheless. I have realised it is impossible for me to remain silent about the state of our world, and the suffering of its people- suffering we have the ability to alleviate without hardship, yet still refuse to remove.

Instead, we sit and watch them suffer; sit and discuss tactics, goals, finance. We refuse to see the reality that the figures we analyse represent real people, and that every three and a half seconds we waste in discussion, another 25,000 children die due to poverty.

We made a promise as a world and must now live to fulfil it. To mark a new millennium, a new era, and a new and better world, one such promise was to end poverty and world hunger – a dream that cannot be brought into reality without your help.

Their blood is on our hands, and they die in our names, since we have the ability to end this madness, but refuse to do so. Instead, we fund for wars, and death and destruction, when it's that very death we should be trying to prevent. Moreover, we must understand that this Millennium Goal will never be achieved if we focus on soothing the effects of hunger, for the real problem will remain and target new victims. No, to end world hunger, we must annihilate its source head on: poverty.

Know that less than 1 per cent of what the world spent every year on weapons was needed to put every child into school by the year 2000, and yet it didn't happen. The fact that these children have no education means they will be trapped in poverty, thus unable to pay for food, unable to work as they grow weaker, and then eventually dying from malnutrition simply because they were forced to endure the torment of poverty, when there are already effective programs out there to break this spiral.

... Thus we must let it be so that each dawn brings hope of life instead of death, because starvation takes another soul each time the victims of the world's most devastating nightmare rises from their sleep, unable to dream; for how can one who has never tasted the sweetness of liberation hope for change? But should it be so? We, with our power and money and resources, can reach out to the people of the world and give them what they deserve as a basic human right; the right to eat and drink and live in safety.

... It took one man, did it not, to say that he had a dream; a dream that his children would not be judged by the colour of their skin, but by the content of their character. It took one man to bring down the barriers of black and white, and deliver a speech that changed the world, when it was thought that nothing could end the hostility and discrimination between two races so different yet so similar; accepted that nothing could eradicate lifetimes of mistrust and inequality to provide blacks with an equal status in society. It was thought impossible. But look to today, where the first black man is elected as the President of the United States of America.

So why are we so afraid to push for change once more – not as one man or woman, but as a world? You, world leaders, have the power to end one of the greatest afflictions suffered by humanity.... So why do you hesitate to end it now?

James Trouton

Portadown College, Co. Armagh,
Northern Ireland, Age 14

MDG 1 – ERADICATE EXTREME HUNGER AND POVERTY

Mr. President, Mr. Secretary-General, Ladies and Gentlemen,

You sit here today at the United Nations General Assembly with a great opportunity. You my friends could change the world. You my friends could eradicate extreme poverty and hunger in many areas. If that alone isn't enough motivation for you, think of it this way. Your mothers, fathers, brothers, sisters, grandmothers, grandfathers, sons and daughters are living without food or clean water and have done for days on end. They live on below $1 per day but work longer and harder than you or I could ever imagine. Every single day they face chronic hunger. They haven't just skipped a meal. They've been unable to scrape together a meal for many days. Do you mean to tell me that, had this been your loved ones been in this appalling situation you would not have helped with all your ability? Okay, so maybe it isn't your loved ones, but they are someone's and they need help.

Ten years ago you and many others made a solemn promise to the Third World to eradicate extreme poverty and hunger. Now with only five years to go this dream seems as far off an ambition as ever it was. The first target set as a stepping stone to achieving this goal was to reduce by half the proportion of the population living on less than one meagre dollar each day. One single dollar is only enough to buy a handful of small sweets and these people are made to live on less than that while you drive around in your swish cars; at least though you are here with an open mind, and hopefully a willing heart. A staggering 13 per cent of the world's population live on this miniscule amount. One such example is Soa. Soa is a woman from Diego in Madagascar. She has five children, the youngest of which is six years old. Their father died six months ago and now Soa sells tea, coffee and rice cakes on the streets for only 2.5p each. This is her only source of income and she struggles to feed all seven of them on this money. Things are so hard for her that a gift of €8.00 brought tears to her eyes. The most heart wrenching thing of all is that there are many more people like Soa, millions in fact. You sit here today with a chance to end this suffering, to put things right. You can help, you must help.

… All of these targets will need much effort and many donations. You people here are in a wonderful position to give this money and help to those much worse off than yourselves. The question tonight my friends is not, "Can you?" It is, "Will you?" I look at your faces here and you are all obviously touched by the plight of these people, and rightly so. I plead with you to help. Many lives will be lost every minute, every hour, every day you put off from helping. I've done all I can, now it's over to you.

Stephen Conn

Portadown College, Co. Armagh,
Northern Ireland, Age 15

MDG 1 – ERADICATE EXTREME POVERTY AND HUNGER

Presidents, Kings and Queens, Prime Ministers and Honoured Guests, I have been invited here to speak to you today about some very important issues. Five years to go until your promises will be broken. As you will all know, in 2000 world leaders, some who are in this room today, made eight solemn promises to the developing world: "The Millennium Goals". We all know that now is the time to act to meet these targets. We may not meet all these goals, but we are going to make progress and fast. I am going to talk to you, my esteemed friends, about only one of these goals though: child poverty and hunger.

Rubbish and landfill sites. The amount of food we waste in the developed world is unbelievable. We sit in our warm cosy homes, or treat ourselves to a meal at a lush restaurant and we complain about a slightly burnt chip. Now let's think about the poor and underprivileged. They wake up in the morning with nothing waiting for them to eat. They have to scavenge like rats for the next meal. They do not know were it is going to come from. We often see pictures of children searching in piles of rubbish which are full of diseases and nasty surprises for the scraps. I ask you, is this ethical? Is it fair? Poverty is without doubt an awful thing and it hits children the hardest. A sever lack of products and services hurts ever human being, but it is most threatening to children's rights: survival, health and nutrition and education to name a few. Poverty creates an environment that is damaging to a child's development physically, mentally, emotionally and spiritually. So these deprivations greatly hamper children's ability to achieve their full potential. They are too weak to go to school and their greatest worry is the next meal, thus contributing to a society's cycle of endless poverty and hunger. We need to help more children get to school as it is a child's strongest defence against poverty. Educated girls are more likely to marry later and have healthier children helping to curb the cycle. Poverty exacerbates the effects of HIV/AIDS and armed conflict. They have little chance of surviving to their teens. 300 million children go to bed every day hungry. Only eight per cent of them are victims of famine or other emergency situations. Truly shocking. This has just got to stop. It is horrendous and sickening that in the twenty-first century there age still children struggling so much. These children are being robbed of their basic rights.

... One-two-three: In the last 10 seconds three people have died of starvation. Usually it is a child under the age of five. That's eighteen million per year or an astonishing 50,000 per day. This was not my vision of 2010; was it yours? When we can act we must, no arguments. If we don't then I'm sorry to tell you this, but their blood is on my and your hands. That is not what you want, is it? No, just as I thought.

Emma Rutter

Friends School, Lisburn, Co. Antrim,
Northern Ireland, Age 12

MDG 1 – ERADICATE EXTREME POVERTY AND HUNGER

I sit in the cold, staring at the stars. My belly aches with hunger and I feel the pangs rush through me, each one of them hurting worse than the one before until it is so bad I could almost pass out. But I do not. I am strong, for this has happened to me all before – many times, more than I could care to count. I have not ever known a day when I have not had to scrounge for food, picking at dustbins outside restaurants and houses. I have not ever known a day without seeing yet another person dead, twitching on the street, and each day I thank God that it wasn't me.

Everyone else I had, everyone else I used to trust, is now dead. Father was the first to go, then Chandra and Takiko. Finally Mama went, although it was no easy rest for her. If I fall asleep here, now, anywhere, I am still haunted in my dreams by her screeches and frequent clutching at figures in the air, figures that didn't even exist. I hope she is happy now, wherever she may be. I hope she looks at me and thinks that she is proud, proud that I have lasted so long without anyone's help.

My stomach growls again, demanding food, water, some sort of nourishment. I am so used to it now that I do not notice it; it has become such a part of me.

But this time; this time is different. The pain is so bad tears squeeze out from behind my eyes, no matter how much I try to keep them in. I slump against the wall and pull my thin t-shirt around me, challenging the wind to do its worst. I see it now; the rising swoops and gusts of air, blowing rubbish and who-knows-what-else down through the alleys and twisting side streets of my town, the town I have lived in ever since I was a baby, and the town that I know every corner of.

I hug my t-shirt tighter, knowing I should feel something, some sort of cold air, but I don't. It scares me, not having my senses; it feels like some part of me is missing. Then suddenly Mama appears; and Chandra and Takiko and Father too. They are smiling at me, sat round a table with five places set. All are filled – except one. I know that place is for me, and I realise what is happening – my time has come. I am frightened; the death that I have fought off for so long has finally come to claim me. I push against it – I don't want to go but it is hopeless. The table gets closer, filling my line of vision until it is all I can see. Bright plates filled with sandwiches, seafood, sausages and thousands more delicacies that I never even knew existed. They become so bright, so loud and colourful it hurts my eyes. I close them, willing to be free, and the everlasting sleep takes me.

This, leaders, is the consequence of poverty. No doubt you already know that – but I hope to put a fresh spin on this dangerous and widespread issue.

... Food is like oxygen – every human needs it to survive. It is possible to go for some days without it but it cannot be for long. Poverty-stricken people are an example of this – many of them die before reaching their first birthday, and many more die before their second birthday. That is a shocking fact, when compared to the number of people in the Western World who will live on till their eightieth or even ninetieth birthday.

Just ponder these thoughts I have put to you. Think about how Aalap (the above character) will have felt when he passed away. And think of how much you and I have compared to them. Think of how hungry they must all be.

But most importantly, think of what you can do to change it.

Orla Lenehen

St. Thomas Aquinas School, Birmingham,
United Kingdom, Age 15

MDG 6 – COMBAT HIV/AIDS, MALARIA AND OTHER DISEASES"

… I am going to take you on a journey, far from the comfort of this large building, the hustle and bustle of daily life. Where at the end of a hard day's work you'll probably go home to your loved ones, have dinner, and perhaps complain about the large workload. You sit down in front of the television and see stories on the news, which may shock you at the time, but a few hours later, they are, perhaps, the furthest thing from your mind.

One million lives taken every year, and for what? Malaria, which is a preventable and curable disease, takes the lives of 3,000 children in Africa every day. That's a life lost every 30 seconds, enough women and children to fill seven jumbo jets each day.

I find it strange how, in the developed world, people can be truly devastated when a celebrity marriage breaks down, or there is an argument between two well-known figures. There's a huge outcry from the public, so much so, that people even take sides, part of "Team This" or "Team That". It's a shame there isn't this compassionate, this drive, for the millions of children affected by malaria. If millions of people were dying every year in the developed world, the Governments would seek out the problem, and stop it, as soon as possible. Just because the problem is not on our doorsteps, does not mean it is non-existent. Mr. Lance Laifer, a hedge fund manager from New Jersey, started researching malaria two and a half years ago. He said: "One of the lessons from the Holocaust was not to allow preventable deaths. We can stomach this because it doesn't happen to our neighbours, to our kids."

I recently had an experience I will never forget in a hospital in Ethiopia.

I visited many of the wards, and saw some pretty horrendous, awful sights. I came to this one ward, where this young girl, Marie, was being treated. Her family came from a remote part of Africa, and it had taken them three hours to get to the hospital on foot. She was suffering from severe dehydration, and had a high fever. She needed a blood transfusion, and quickly. The doctors and nurses were doing all they could. I exited the room for ten minutes or so to get some fresh air. When I returned to, I found what looked like a bundle of dirty sheets on the bed. However, this was not the case. It was the small, four-year-old's body. Marie had died. In the space of ten minutes, this young girl's battle against malaria had been lost. I continued my tour around the hospital, that image of Marie haunting me. I remember we came across this one peaceful room, full of sleeping children, at least twenty. It was almost like a place to escape the dreadful things I had witnessed in the other wards. That was, of course, until the doctor who was showing me around told me the children weren't sleeping; they were all in malaria comas. Many would never wake up, never leave that hospital.

"For the want of £5, a net was lost. For the want of a net, a life was lost. For the want of that life, all hope was lost." You may recognise this to be a rephrased version of the well-known proverb, "for the want of a nail". It seems ridiculous, that for the same price as an evening dinner for a family of four, a life could be saved. £5 can buy a mosquito net, for prevention of the disease. Just 80p can buy emergency medicine, which could have saved Marie, and so many young boys and girls just like her. Economist Jeffrey Sachs estimates that it will cost $3 billion a year to eradicate malaria; the equivalent of two days of the Pentagon's spending. It's almost laughable, that for so little, millions of innocent lives could be saved each year.

Deirbhile Craven

Our Lady's Grammar School,
Newry, Co. Down, Age 14

MDG 4 – REDUCE CHILD MORTALITY

In the UK, the average person lives to see 70 or 80. but in Africa one in six children don't live to see five. This cannot be allowed to go on. We in the developed world know what is happening but seem to continue to accept it.

In Sierra Leone and Afghanistan a child is 87 times more likely to die than one born in Sweden. We need to ask ourselves why this is happening and what can be done about it. There is no doubt that poverty has a major impact in these countries. In all the countries with high mortality rates poor education standards and poor sanitation is widespread. If mothers were educated on how to make simple changes to their living conditions infection would be lower and more children would survive.

This is not just about throwing money at the problem. However the fact still remains that hunger and malnutrition are the biggest causes of child mortality in developing countries. Six million children die each year as a result of hunger, which is one child dying every five seconds. What this does prove though is most of the deaths *are* preventable and that all we need is a little bit of effort and finance. We are not asking for huge changes in technology, as most lives could be saved by low-tech, relatively cheap measures such as vaccines, antibiotics, bed nets and improved family care.

The World Health Organisation makes every effort to help people in these poor countries and to spread the word to the likes of us that help is needed. It doesn't mean breaking the bank; it just means giving that £2 to charity instead of buying that extra cup of coffee or magazine. If people knew that it took such little effort to make such a big change, then surely more people would offer to help. We need you to spread the word that help is needed along with the work you are doing.

Centuries ago countries like ours experienced child mortality rates that the likes of African countries are experiencing now. If we managed to change the way our country works, why can't we change theirs? It may have taken centuries to change our country, but these people do not have centuries to spare. Unless we do something about this now, millions of children are going to suffer unnecessarily.

... The United Nations' goal to reduce the amount of child mortality by two-thirds by 2015 cannot be reached unless we all work together. All the world leaders need to get together and sort this out – after all, there are only five years left to achieve this goal. We need to do a lot more work in these next five years than we have done in the previous ten years if we want to make a difference.

Aditi Upmanyu

Maharaja Sawai Mansingh Vidyalaya,
Jaipur, India, Age 15

MDG 4 – REDUCE CHILD MORTALITY

... Louis Pasteur once said: "When I approach a child, he inspires in me two sentiments; tenderness for what he is, and respect for what he may become." But unfortunately, not many of the kids born every year survive to even dream about what they may become. The number of increasing infant mortality rates in developing nations doesn't seem to curb. Children are often considered as a country's biggest resource and ironically the governments of Less Developed Countries (LDCs) fail to provide the infants and their families a hygienic ambience and proper health and sanitation facilities. Isn't it a matter of great shame for any country and for us too?

… It's deplorable to know that nine out of ten women have their deliveries done at home in Ethiopia in unhygienic conditions, either because of illiteracy or because of no accessibility and affordability to proper delivery processes. Many infants are prematurely delivered and this fact constitutes to another big reason of infant mortality. We must seek to employ well-trained gynaecologists and arrange hospitals with well equipped and advanced labs to carry out safe delivery processes. Health checkups for infant and mother should be conducted regularly.

The famous Indian writer and poet, Rabindranath Tagore, quoted that every child comes with the message that God is not yet discouraged of man. Yet when a child dies even before learning to speak or walk, it leaves me suspicious of the fact that God is not yet discouraged of man. But He is not to be blamed. We have to be blamed. If we all are unwavering in controlling the growing infant mortality rate, it's no more a hazy blur. Let's pledge today to enforce all our discussed ideas into immediate actions in order to nurture the best within the world's future generation.

Iona Teague

Henry Beaufort School, Winchester,
Hampshire, UK, Age 15

MDG 4 – REDUCE CHILD MORTALITY

Ten years is a long time. In ten years, a tiny, innocent baby can grow and mature into an intelligent child. In ten years, useless wasteland can be transformed into a fully-functional, booming city. In ten years, inordinate technological and medical discoveries can be made that have the potential to change the world forever.

A decade ago, the respectable people that call themselves our heads of state made eight solemn promises to the developing world. These statements gave us, the rich, powerful, fortunate Europeans to help others who, through absolutely no fault of their own, find themselves in tremendously frightful and appalling situations. What kind, generous people we are.

Naturally, it does not take a fool to comprehend what an immensely gargantuan task eradicating extreme hunger and poverty is, and what complications such actions would pose. No amount of cynical sarcasm or doubtful irony can truly erase the underlying enormity of the tasks proposed; these promises were certainly not going to be easy to fulfil. Such bold and certain promises that fill the hearts of countless people with hope and proposed escape simply must be followed by obvious action, otherwise faith and hope – essential aspects of any radical changes – will evaporate.

I assure you, I am not an ungrateful adolescent, and I *am* able to understand and humbly acknowledge the excessive exertion and energy that has been involved concerning achieving this particular goal.

Perhaps it is a mere figment of my "over-processed, over-dramatic, over-worked teenage brain", but it appears that there are still rather a lot of people on this swarming planet that are diseased, starving and meagre. Words are simply incapable of describing the immense desperateness of their dire situations. No food, no home, no life. Eradicated? I think not.

At least eighty per cent of humanity live on less than ten dollars a day. That is about as much pocket money I get a week. The poorest forty per cent of the world's population accounts for five percent of global income; the richest twenty per cent account for three-quarters of it.

... I am not here to churn horrific details and reinforce mundane ideas that have been overused to such an extent that they are totally meaningless to any soul who possesses any actual power to change them. I am here to reinforce the raw truth that is behind these plain, inked statistics. These numbers are people. Real people. People like you and me, people with hopes, dreams, ambitions and fears.

... You have five years left, rest assured, *I* will be counting. However, I can guarantee those who you promised to help will not be – they have all given up hope by now.

Eimear Duff

Dominican College, Whitehall, Dublin, Ireland, Age 15

MDG 3 – Promote Gender Equality and Empower Women

I, like most girls in the first world, am fortunate enough to have been bestowed with the gifts of equality, empowerment and education: fruits of the labour of those before me who believed that women should have the same rights as men, who never abandoned hope that their ideals could be realised, despite numerous obstacles. Previous generations in my family teach me that girls were not always treated fairly. My grandmother had to leave school early to help her mother with housework, while her brothers were allowed to continue their education. When she got married, law and the etiquette of society forced her to quit her job. Looking after her growing family became her sole job description.

Bit by bit, things improved: creeping cracks were seen in the glass ceiling. All of my grandmother's six children had equal rights and the same standard of education, regardless of gender. Her daughters were free to choose their varied career paths; one would become a doctor, another a solicitor, the next an engineer, and my mother a teacher. Later, upon marrying and having children, her daughters continued to work. And so I came into existence: born a girl, a fact that gave delight, not disappointment, to my parents. I was not aborted. I was not treated with hate and scorn as being worthless, a liability to be married off. I was not sold, or put up for adoption: I was equal.

Unfortunately, although many in the first world take it for granted, equality for women is not a universal truth. Though the target of the third MDG was to eliminate gender disparity all levels of education, after a decade the fact remains that two-thirds of children being denied primary education are girls. Inequalities are also seen in politics, where less than one out of every five parliamentarians is a woman.

We cannot expect to reach any of the MDGs when half the world's population, half its potential, is being ignored and marginalised. Investing in the education and status of girls and women has effects that never die. Educated and healthy women benefit their families, communities and countries. An educated mother will be able to release her children from the chains of poverty and hunger, a land title and inheritance will increase her status and wealth to dramatically improve her and her children's prospect.

Ladies and Gentlemen, gender equality is not just another one of the eight Millennium Development Goals; it is a fundamental human right. We need to give girls a voice, so that their children may one day have the opportunity to speak before you, and thank you. Let us create a world where "it's a girl" becomes a proclamation of joy, not a life sentence. Let us achieve universal gender equality and change the course of history. After all, history is *herstory* too.

Jennifer Gaule

Laurel Hill Colaiste, Limerick, Ireland, Age 13

MDG 4 – REDUCE CHILD MORTALITY

… You may wonder why I feel so strongly about this but as you are all aware, Ireland suffered from its own tragic famine in which millions of people died. This inspired me to speak to you about child mortality. Everyday seeing babies and children dying on the television, I wonder how much is being done about it. It is now 2010. I feel you have not done enough to ensure your target will be reached.

You cannot afford to break your promise; the Third World is depending on it.

We need to ask ourselves, "why are these children and babies dying?" They are dying because of malnutrition, malaria, measles, pneumonia, diarrhoea, neglect, abandonment, and lack of hygiene, sanitation and medicine. Two-thirds of these deaths are preventable.

Why are they dying from malnutrition? There is enough food in the world, isn't there? There is enough food in the world but Mother Nature causes droughts, floods, tornados and earthquakes which destroy crops in the Third World. Since 1992 food scarcity that can be attributed to human causes, has almost doubled going from 15 per cent to 35 per cent. If the toddlers and babies are mal-nourished they are less immune to disease and are less likely to survive. Around 60 per cent of children die because of hunger. Hunger and malnutrition kills more people than AIDS, TB and malaria combined. To solve this desperate problem that many face every day of their lives, in the short term you have to increase the food aid going to these countries. In the long term, you must provide these countries with seeds for crops and the knowledge to tend to these so as to provide food for the young and needy.

Why are they dying from pneumonia and other diseases when children in the first world countries would survive? The reason is because the first world is charging the Third World countries the same amount for medicine as they would charge other First World countries. Then the Third World countries can't afford the medicine. We need to charge Third World countries less because how else can they afford to treat their babies and toddlers when they are sick, when they have barely any money to live on at any rat?. They need to have their babies vaccinated against diseases so they will be stronger. We can save millions of toddlers and chil-dren every year by introducing oral rehydration therapy for chil-dren with diarrhoea ...

Corey McClean

Monkstown Community School, Newtownabbey, Northern Ireland, Age 13

MDG 1 – ERADICATE EXTREME POVERTY AND HUNGER

… In 1998, $8 billion was spent on cosmetics in the USA, $11 billion was spent on ice cream in Europe, $12 billion was spent on perfumes in Europe and the USA and $17 billion was spent on pet food in Europe and the USA.

We spend all that money on unnecessary items, while the cost of basic education for all the children in developing countries is $6 billion, for water and sanitation for all in developing countries is $9 billion, $12 billion for reproductive health for all the women in developing countries and $13 billion for health and nutrition.

We are spending this ridiculous amount of money on unnecessary items and not on items which are extremely necessary; we really have to make a move soon.

How can we call them developing countries when they are not developing at all? These countries are stuck in a poverty trap and we need to help them help themselves. I am only a 13-year-old girl, yet I can see how the richer are getting richer and the poorer are getting poorer. We in the Developed World are blind to the destruction we are causing to the planet. We are using up all the natural resources and are making it impossible for the poorest of the poor to have any hope.

This is a clear case of man's inhumanity to man.

Lucy Dudman

Oathall Community College,
West Sussex, England, Age 15

MDG 1 – ERADICATE EXTREME POVERTY AND HUNGER

I am here to speak to you not as a stranger, but as a friend. Thus, I trust you will listen to me today as I am fighting for what is right. I have come here to denounce the predicament that still hangs over the world like a dark cloud; it is something that still menaces those who die quietly in some of the poorest villages on earth. It is something that has a palpable sense of urgency: Poverty.

Poverty is fundamentally immoral. Is it fair that over one-third of deaths are caused by extreme malnourishment and unspeakable conditions? I have come here to speak out in a plea for the United Nations to come together and do what they exist for – bring people together to work for peace and development and achieve rightful justice and well-being for all. No longer shall we stay silent in the face of poverty; you and I must strive to help disadvantaged people lead better lives and eliminate the spread of disease and illiteracy.

If current trends continue, the Millennium Development Goals' solemn promise of halving the proportion of underweight children will be missed. If trends continue, we will effectively be ignoring every second child who is stricken by poverty. Is ignorance an enviable trait? I am forced to assume that the rest of the world is either too ignorant to accept this harsh realism, or they have fallen victim to the inundation of statistics and images of poverty that make us all believe this is an unalterable state of affairs. Let me tell you that it is not unalterable, but eradicating poverty still remains to be one of the main, moral challenges of our time.

It is vital that today we set the course for the world's efforts to alleviate poverty by 2015. Let me remind you that we have five years left. If this cannot be accomplished, all hope of helping our fellow men, women and children will slip right from our very fingertips and will crash to the ground with incredible force as billions of lives will have just been shattered by the failure of the UN.

... In our own hands lies the power to abolish all forms of human poverty as the world now stands at the halfway point towards making the goals a reality. There is reason for optimism. We have already begun to make a change to a country that sixteen years ago had a completely devastated economy and infrastructure due to the genocide. I would like to bring to your attention again, Rwanda, a country now benefiting from a period of relative security and stability. I have a vision – a wonderful vision – that Rwanda will one day be a prosperous place, relying on no one but themselves. Let me tell you that any improvements in any country will always be music to my ears.

Kelly Skillen

Our Lady's Grammar, Newry, Co. Down,
Northern Ireland, Age 14

MDG 4 – REDUCE CHILD MORTALITY

... Even if there have been improvements, it is still not enough to reach our goal. We should take heed from the Eritrean government in Northeast Africa. They launched an aggressive vaccination campaign to help reduce child mortality. They vaccinated 76 per cent of children in 2002, which is a massive increase from 9.6 per cent in 1991. They also trained 500 additional healthcare workers in the Integrated Management of Childhood Illness. They look carefully at the lives of children and infants and gather information to help them save their children and even with these impressive results, they still feel they haven't done enough and want to do more to help. I am sure you will agree that any successful methods, such as the Eritrean government's, should be introduced into countries that still need more help to save their children.

In other countries there are improvements in key child-survival interventions. These include vitamin A supplementation, insecticide-treated bed nets, exclusive breastfeeding, vaccinations and wider coverage of HIV interventions. HIV interventions also include treatment of pregnant mothers to stop the virus spreading to their baby. Vaccination for measles has now reached 82 per cent of the worlds children and there has been a dramatic decrease of 74 per cent of measles related deaths. There are also second chance vaccinations for children who missed vaccinations.

I am sure that if these methods were introduced into countries that need help, then this would definitely help us reach our goal ...

Amy Tate

Portadown College, Co. Armagh,
Northern Ireland, Age 15

MDG 2 – ACHIEVE UNIVERSAL PRIMARY EDUCATION

... The goal of a primary education for every child, along with the seven others, is supposed to be realised in five years time. If it is going to happen then drastic measures need to be taken – right here and now – at full steam ahead. We have made promises to our equals in these developing countries. Are we going to short change them? I do hope not! Let's, quite simply, make education freely available to one and all.

Imagine this. A child, aged sixteen, from a developed country, has never really been interested in school. He doesn't try in class and doesn't complete any of his home works. He is constantly in detention. His teachers are continuously contacting his parents. Nothing makes any difference. When his GCSE results come out they are unsatisfactory and, so, he has to leave school.

Picture this other scenario. A child, aged sixteen, from a developing country, has dreamed about going to school. When she is older, she longs to be a primary school teacher and help other children in the same situation as she was in. Unfortunately, her parents haven't got the money to send her to school and, so, she can't make her dreams a reality.

In developed countries, by law, children have to attend school until they are sixteen. Their education is free. Some young people take it for granted. They hate school and see it as a waste of time. They can't wait to opt out and do so as soon as they have had their sixteenth birthday – often not completing their Year 12.

Why then, are these ready and willing children from developing countries denied an education and, hand in hand with it, the chance of a better life for themselves and their families?

The main reason there are high illiteracy rates in developing countries is that government education is not free and parents quite simply cannot afford to send their children to school. As they can't afford to pay for contraception, even if they know what it is, as well as the high infant mortality rate, they have large families and, so, struggle to feed them, let alone educate them.

It's not the case that they don't value education. They, just like us, want the very best for their children. They want for them the chances that they never had – an education and, with it, a better way of life. They are well aware that schooling is vital for their kids if they are to break free from the vicious circle of poverty engulfing them …

Mohammed Ali Anasov

Clonburris National School, Clondalkin,
Dublin, Ireland, Age 11

MDG 1 – ERADICATE EXTREME POVERTY AND HUNGER

... Children wake up hungry all over the world .We have breakfast; they do not. We have lunch; they do not .We have dinner; they do not.

We have a choice of food; they might only have a bowl of porridge or rice once a day, if they are lucky.

They have to walk miles to get water; we don't, we just turn on the tap. That water has to last them for two/three days.

These facts made me feel sad .I have a much better life than these children.

I felt I would like to help them. But you can *definitely* help them .You have the *power* to help them.

You can send them money. You can send them animals .You can send them food. With the money they could buy some food for their family. With the animals, they can get milk and they can make cheese. Or they can get yogurt. If they have hens they can get eggs. They can make different types of meals. Their families will be stronger and their parents would be proud.

We collected money from every child in our class. Altogether we collected €60.00. With this money we sent a mother goat, a kid and a flock of chickens. We were very proud of our selves because we helped a family to be independent.

If we have helped one just think how many families can you help?

I hope you will help them.

Aisling Taylor

Laurel Hill Colaiste, Limerick, Ireland, Age 13

MDG 2 – ACHIEVE UNIVERSAL PRIMARY EDUCATION

… I chose this goal because as a student I know how important education is and will be to me when I get older to get a job or to enable me to fulfill my dreams. Education is a valuable resource for me. Every human being should be given the right to develop his/her full potential and achieve his/her goals in life whatever their circumstances.

… A family friend recently spent time in Kenya and when she came home she said that we here in Ireland have a lot to learn from the people there they rely on themselves number one to get on in this world and put their family first above everything else. It reminded her of the animals in the wild they fend for themselves and look after their own to the last. They do not rely on the state to solve their problems.

Although help directed to basic education for low-income countries increased from $1.6 billion in 1999 to $5 billion in 2006, it is still well below the estimated $11 billion in aid needed every year to reach universal primary education by 2015.

I also think we have to stand on our own feet like the Kenyans and not rely on the state to solve our problems the recession in the developed world has proved this. We in the developed world need to know and understand the importance of this Chinese proverb: "Give a man a fish feed him for a day, teach a man to fish and you feed him for life."

If we truly understood this in the developed world the world would be a better place for all and the MDG Achieving Universal Primary education for all children by 2015 would be achieved …

Mark Stewart

St. Columba's College, Lifford,
Co. Donegal, Age 14

MDG 7 – ENSURE ENVIRONMENTAL SUSTAINABILITY

... Goal Seven plays a major part in gender equality as women and girls are often burdened by water and food collection. The diseases that cause child mortality are spread through unclean water and inadequate sanitation. Respiratory infections are a direct result of air pollution. Maternal health would be greatly improved if the air was cleaner and if women did not have to travel far distances for food and water. Major diseases could therefore be wiped out if again they had environmental sustainability.

As you've heard, a lot of the other goals would be achieved much easier if goal number seven was achieved. As you know, the poor who are most dependent on natural resources and are mostly affected by environmental degradation do not always have the access to information, rights, or decisions making and policy development to implement these.

Climate change is a major threat in the developing world. The annual level of rainfall has reduced dramatically as the temperatures continue soar. Did you know that water consumption per person is ten times higher in developed countries than in developing countries? The rate of forestry that was being cut down every year in the 1990s was more than nine million hectares. That is the equivalent of losing 2.4 per cent of the total forested area of the world every year. And 75 per cent of fisheries stock are being exploited at or above their maximum capacity and several have already collapsed due to over-fishing. These are serious problems ...

Ellie Collett

The Cotswold School, Cheltenham, England, Age 13

MDG 4 – REDUCE CHILD MORTALITY

… We need to open our eyes and realise the terrifying and shocking statistic that is staring us in the face. Thirty thousand children, that's how many children died today. But I am going to tell about one. Areta was three years old. She died alone of pneumonia in a little village named Byei, wondering what she had done to deserve this life, and what she had done that meant she deserved to die. She was invisible, more invisible than death itself. She has done nothing wrong. It is not her fault that she died. In a way, it is ours. We did not listen to her cries; we did not tend to her when she needed us the most. We are responsible.

Thirty thousand other children just like Areta died today. Thirty thousand children just like Areta died yesterday, and will die tomorrow, and thirty thousand more the day after that. These children are forgotten, far away from the conscience and scrutiny of the modern world. Left behind in poverty stricken lands where you are lucky to make it to your first birthday, poverty stricken lands where if you become ill, your only hope is to count the days until you either miraculously survive, or die.

But why is this happening? Why has something not been done about it? Why, when providing adequate food, clean water, and basic education for the worlds poorest children can all be achieved for less than what we spend annually on make up, ice cream and pet food, are children still dying of malnutrition and simple diseases the can be cured inexpensively and treated easily?

Not enough is being done …

Toni Upton

Portadown College, Co. Armagh,
Northern Ireland, Age 14

MDG 1 – ERADICATE EXTREME POVERTY AND HUNGER

... From statistical evidence at least 80 per cent of humanity lives on less than $10 dollars a day which would be approximately £6 pounds sterling. Contrast this with the forecast that 2012 Olympic Games in London are already over budget by £900 million which originally was estimated to be between £5 to 20 billion. Where is the justification in these comparisons?

According to UNICEF, 25,000 children die each day due to poverty and a direct quote is: "And they die quietly in some of the poorest villages on earth, far removed from the scrutiny and the conscience of the world. Being meek and weak in life makes these dying multitudes even more invisible in death." Around 27-28 per cent of all children are estimated to be underweight or stunted. Statistics show that the millennium Goal will be missed by 30 million children because of slow progress. It is my belief that the slow progress is a direct result of misuse of the world economy, too much money and resources are being spent on either sporting or cultural events or ill advised war efforts. Government and media frenzies such as the 2009 "swine flu epidemic", where millions of pounds was spent on vaccinations, half of which were unused.

The Millennium Goal is to halve the amount of poverty and hunger, but how can this be reached when people are spending ridiculous amounts on the Olympic Games, new buildings and salaries. In order to reach this goal we should be thinking about the starving people and poverty. Many countries can not afford food, clothes, water or shelter, whilst people like you and I sit at home to three cooked meals a day, heat, money and transport. For us to pour a glass of water from a tap is nothing compared for people in the under developed countries for they have to pump unclean water, carry it for miles, then drink it with the possible risk of infections diseases which can be fatal. So as I stand before you my public I ask of you what would you do to help?

Ladies and Gentlemen how could you cope with living on 50p a day? How would you survive? Could you carry on? Millions of people live their lives on 50p a day and will continue to do so until we can stop poverty and hunger. So again I ask if you could do anything to help, would you? In order to reach our goal we need to improve standards and banish poverty and hunger.

Together we can do it!

SOUNDBITES – JUNIOR

Eireann Moloney

*Presentation Secondary School, Mitchelstown,
Co. Cork, Ireland, Age 14*

MDG 1 – ERADICATE EXTREME POVERTY AND HUNGER

... These are all facts and figures, but what we need isn't the negativity of people saying we will not make the goal. Look at all the progress we have made, people have made a difference and if we make more progress then I believe this goal can be achieved. There are so many children that deserve a chance for a life and they don't even make it to the age of five. It is so hard to imagine this world, of poverty and children dying, but it is out there. Just because we don't see it doesn't mean it isn't real. I thank you for listening to my speech and I hope this has made an impact on how we can do this, we can reduce child mortality.

Nathan Murray

Clonburris National School, Clondalkin, Dublin, Ireland, Age 10

MDG 1 – ERADICATE EXTREME POVERTY AND HUNGER

... In the developed world, we spend $13 billion on perfume every year. This is sufficient to eradicate hunger in the entire world.

Every five seconds a child dies in Africa or South America or India. They die of hunger. It is a disgrace! It is very sad. It is a human disaster.

I would like to speak to you about responsibility. All families should have a proper home, good health, a good life. Everyone has the right to go to school, to eat proper food and to live in a clean, warm house.

Martha Glaser

Lady Margaret Secondary School, London, England, Age 13

MDG 2 – ACHIEVE UNIVERSAL PRIMARY EDUCATION

Firstly, I am sure you all know that constantly supplying aid is simply *not* the way to eradicate extreme poverty and hunger. We need developing countries to be self-sufficient, to grow, and to prosper, not to depend on our aid. By investing some of our well-earned money into building new schools in third-world countries, we are immediately opening the doors to a life of achieved ambitions and a better future for these children. They will grow up to become doctors, lawyers, and perhaps even teachers, who will pass on their knowledge to other eager students. These educated children will come to provide an excellent income for their families – and who knows, maybe in a few decades time, these children will be sitting in our places, and deciding on the future of our world?

Dáire Brown

Our Lady's Grammar School, Newry,
Co. Down, Northern Ireland, Age 14

MDG 4 – REDUCE CHILD MORTALITY

This tells us that the children in this world do not need us to empathise with them; they need us to help them have a better and longer life. They need solutions and today in this world, we not only have the financial resources to end extreme poverty once and for all, but we have the technological knowledge to stop it. It is also clear, however, that is we carry on in a "business as usual" mode, the goals will not be achieved by 2015. The way forward is marked; it is only the political will to achieve the goals that is in question. One thing that is known is that mortality rates are higher for children from rural and poor families and whose mothers lack a basic education.

Sharon Greaney

Méanscoil Nua an Leitriúigh, Tralee,
Co. Kerry, Ireland, Age 14

MDG 1 – Eradicate Extreme Poverty and Hunger

World Leaders of today we need your help to put an end to this horrific tragedy. Together along with the help and dedication of the rest of the world I believe that we can reach the ambitious goal of eradicating world poverty and hunger, and achieve what many have failed to do. I will leave you now with a famous quote:

> *"The day that hunger is eradicated from the earth, there will be the greatest spiritual explosion the world has ever known. Humanity cannot imagine the joy that will burst in to the world on the day of that great revolution."* – Federico Garcia Lorca, Spanish poet and dramatist.

Eimear Millane

Laurel Hill Coláiste, Limerick, Ireland, Age 12

MDG 1 – Eradicate Extreme Poverty and Hunger

I speak to you as a 12-year-old girl who has just finished her primary education in Ireland. In doing so I realise how fortunate I am, what a chance I've been given. But Ladies and Gentlemen, imagine if I had been born in Africa, what chance would I have there? Would I have the privilege of addressing you? Would I have the words to do so? I believe I would most likely not.

In my view the easiest promise to fulfil is the first one – to halve the amount of people who die from hunger and poverty. One part of the world suffers from the overproduction of beef, lamb and dairy produce and where the most prominent disease results from over-eating thereby causing heart disease and obesity. The situation is little short of ridiculous. Could not the surplus of food from one part of the world be transported to the third world where lack of food intake is the principal cause of death?

Pierce Cambay

St. Conleth's College, Dublin, Ireland, Age 12

MDG 7 – ENSURE ENVIRONMENTAL SUSTAINABILITY

If you think that hunger in Africa is the biggest problem in the world right now, you are horribly wrong. If we don't start reducing our production of greenhouse gases, soon the whole world will be lacking food and sanitation, and then you will realise that solving the problem of global warming is more important than everything else. But then it will be too late, and you will be thinking to yourself, maybe we should have listened to that boy who was trying to help us, maybe we should have tried to change the world ...

Sarah Apsey

Lady Margaret Secondary School,
London, England, Age 13

MDG 5 – IMPROVE MATERNAL HEALTH

Traditionally, the woman's role is predominantly domestic, although this has drastically improved in recent years; however, there are still clear divides in the equality between genders. It cannot be disputed that women play the main part in childbirth and as a result men have more opportunity and a higher level of respect in society, as they are able to pursue careers. Thinking about MDG 3, I would like to raise the point that if men were the child bearers, would they receive better health care than that of women currently? If gender equality were to be achieved, then in turn, health care could be improved ...

Aimee Kerr

Our Lady's Grammar School, Newry,
Co. Armagh, Northern Ireland, Age 14

MDG 1 – ERADICATE EXTREME POVERTY AND HUNGER

I believe because we have given ourselves 15 years to achieve this we keep putting it off and thinking we have plenty of time. However in reality we don't and if we are going to meet the target we really need to get our act together!

I'm not totally criticising what has been done I do understand that there are many charities out there and schemes that have tried their best, but I do think that more people need to take part and that governments need to encourage support. I know if we all work hard enough, we will achieve this goal, it is possible!

Dayna Devlin

Clonburris National School, Clondalkin,
Dublin, Ireland, Age 9

MDG 1 – ERADICATE EXTREME POVERTY AND HUNGER

… One-third of the world is well-fed, one third is under-fed and one third is starving. This is very sad to hear. It is possible to change these facts. It is possible to make them history, let's do it before it is too late.

People in Malawi only have one bowl of nsima a day. We have three meals and snacks as well. I suggest you get off your bottoms and travel to Africa and try to help. Is it fair for 24,000 people to die of hunger a day, to be sick and sad and unhealthy? No it is not!!

You must act fast to stop these unnecessary, dreadful deaths. It is a tragedy on a massive scale. We are comfortable, we are washed, we are well-fed. Children in Chad and Uganda and Zimbabwe are not!

In schools in Chechnya and Kosovo children have to learn where to step and where not to step because there are landmines everywhere. Children could lose an arm or a leg if they step on these. That is disgraceful.

We learned all these facts and more when we did a project for Irish Aid on hunger.

Part Two

SENIOR CATEGORY
(16–18 years old)

Extract from speech given by
UN Secretary-General Kofi Annan

Millennium Summit, September 2000

...In an age when human beings have learned the code of human life and can transmit their knowledge in seconds from one continent to another, no mother in the world can understand why her child should be left to die of malnutrition or preventable disease. No one can understand why they should be driven from their home, or imprisoned and tortured for expressing their beliefs. No one can understand why the soil their parents tilled has turned to desert or why their skills have become useless and their family is left hungry. People know that these challenges cannot be met by one country alone, or by government alone. Change cannot be held back by frontiers. Human progress has always come from individual and local initiatives, freely devised and then freely adapted elsewhere.

Your job as political leaders is to encourage such initiatives, to make sure that they are not stifled and that all your peoples can benefit from them, and to limit, or compensate for, the adverse effects that change always has on some people, somewhere.

First Place – Senior

Emer Jones

Presentation Secondary School,
Tralee, Co. Kerry, Ireland, Age 16

MDG 5 – Improve Maternal Health

Mr. President, Mr. Secretary-General, Ladies and Gentlemen,

In Ireland, we have a saying, "*Ní neart go cur le chéile*". This is one of the most well-known and fundamental of our native proverbs. It states that "there is no strength without unity", or "united we stand, divided we fall". Isn't this what the United Nations, or indeed, all of humanity, is about? It is what makes the human race unique; it is what makes the United Nations such a crucial, fundamental and successful part of modern society. It is, in essence, what the Millennium Development Goals aim to achieve: the entire global community working together to make the world a better place.

I am delighted and deeply honoured to have the opportunity to speak today about the Fifth Millennium Development Goal, namely, "to reduce by three-quarters, between 1990 and 2015, the maternal mortality ratio and the proportion of births attended by skilled health personnel and to achieve universal access to reproductive health". This is probably the least globally publicised goal, but is a crucial goal as it directly affects the lives of millions of women and their families across the globe.

Let us rewind a little, to events in September 2000. In this very hall, the United Nations Millennium Declaration, comprising the aims and targets of the Millennium Development Goals, was officially ratified by 187 member states. It was a defining moment in the twenty-first century. It was the beginning of a new millennium, the dawn of a new era; an era of change and optimism for the future. Hopes and dreams were high, expectations and aspirations were promising, the worldwide community was collectively filled with ambition. The Millennium Development Goals, which addressed eight of the world's most challenging yet critical problems, were born from this surge of hope. They gave clear and distinctive targets to work towards; targets which would require a huge amount of international co-operation, determination and generosity to achieve, yet targets which would be achievable and which would greatly impact the lives of so many for the better. Therefore, plans and policies were drawn up, international partnerships were developed and strengthened, and people worldwide rolled into action. The old Irish proverb was truly brought to life.

A decade later, and with just five years left in which to meet the targets of the Millennium Development Goals, where are we today? Did all of those hopes and ambitions just remain as aspirations? Have the countless plans, policies and promises transpired to be the foundation of great progress, the foundation of the improvement of many people's lives throughout the world? I am proud to be a citizen of the world when I say, "Yes, we have made a difference!" We have brought about change for the better, we have implemented policies and the lives of millions of our fellow brothers and sisters in developing countries have improved. During the past decade, the Millennium Declaration and the Millennium Development Goals have led to unprecedented commitments and partnerships reaffirmed in successive summits and meetings. We have shown that we, as a global community, can achieve huge results. You, the world leaders, your governments, people working in humanitarian organisations both big and small, people in rural communities, towns, cities all over the world – we have all united in a common goal to make our world a better place and to increase the living standards and quality of life of millions of people ... and we have succeeded.

However, despite the many successes, overall progress has been too slow for most of the goals to be met by 2015. Many people's lives have changed for the better; many illnesses have been prevented, many deaths have been saved, many opportunities have been afforded to those who had none. But there are still millions, billions, of lives yet to be transformed. The fifth Millennium Development Goal, to drastically reduce maternal mortality, has had the lowest progress rate of the eight goals. Maternal mortality declined only marginally, from 480 deaths per 100,000 live births in 1990 to 450 in 2005. Bear in mind, that the target of the Millennium Development Goal is just 120 deaths per 100,000 live births by 2015. The facts, figures and statistics are shocking. In Sub-Saharan Africa women have a one-in-sixteen chance of death during pregnancy or childbirth. Compare this to the maternal mortality rate in the developed world: just one in 3,800. Only 1 per cent of maternal deaths occur in the developed world; more than 500,000 women in developing countries die every year in childbirth. These statistics are far more than just a number – each figure relates to real people; our brothers and sisters across the globe.

Just think, for a moment, of the devastation maternal mortality causes: children are raised without a mother, husbands lose their wives, friends and family have to cope with the loss of a loved one, as well as trying to survive in the meagre conditions in which they live. I'm sure you will all agree, that it must be a nightmare, a living hell – despite the fact that most of these deaths are completely unnecessary and could easily be prevented.

Major causes of maternal mortality are bacterial infection, unsafe abortions, poor nutrition and medical care, and labour complications. All of these conditions are easily treatable; however, just getting to the nearest clinic to receive proper care in developing nations is often the simple reason why deaths occur. Travelling to and back from the clinic may be very difficult and costly, especially to poor families when time could have been used for working and providing incomes. Even if one reaches the clinic, it may not provide adequate care because of the lack of staff and equipment. In March 2000, a woman in southern Mexico performed a Caesarian section on herself using a kitchen knife – she had a very difficult labour and didn't want her child to die. The nearest clinic was 50 miles away. Unbelievably, both mother and child survived. I felt shivers going up my spine when I first heard about that incident – as I am sure you feel now. Such a horrific event truly highlights the necessity of immediate action to reach the Millennium Development Goal of achieving universal access to reproductive healthcare, as soon as humanly possible. As part of broader investment in public health programmes, adequate financing for maternal health is critical.

Consider the case of India. In 2006, one woman died every five minutes giving birth, often due to poor health, unsafe home births and inadequate access to quality healthcare. More than 100,000 women die every year due to childbirth-related causes. However, over the last four years, the percentage of deliveries assisted by skilled birth attendants increased by more than 30 per cent. Entire communities have actively become involved, for example, with a boost in voluntary blood donations for use during obstetric emergencies. As shown in India, real progress is achievable; it simply requires cooperation, determination and community spirit.

The developed nations of the world can give aid and assistance to developing nations, but it is vital to keep the ancient Chinese proverb in mind: "Give a man a fish and feed him for a day; teach a man to fish and you feed him for a lifetime." The Rose Project is a wonderful example. It aids progress in maternal healthcare in Malawi by providing financial aid, a partnership with well-established Irish maternity hospitals, and proper facilities. It empowers the Malawian people to help themselves; it trains Malawian nurses and midwives and, crucially, encourages them to stay in Malawi, rather than emigrating. All eight Millennium Development Goals are inextricably linked together – an advance in one goal leads to advances in other goals. The opposite is also true: attempts to advance in just one goal without taking the bigger picture into account is not an optimal solution.

Mr. President, Mr. Secretary-General, Ladies and Gentlemen, I thank you most sincerely for allowing me this platform to address you, as one young woman, on behalf of the women of the world. Today, I am appealing to you, our world leaders, to become more concerned about the real impact of the Millennium Development Goals, and to reinvigorate the sense of hope and ambition which was present at the dawn of the millennium. Small communities can work to improve their quality of life, but first they need that lifeline of aid and assistance from the developed nations of the world – from me and from you! Helen Keller once said: "I am only one, but still I am one. I cannot do everything, but still I can do something." This applies to me, but also to each and every one of you. The target date to achieve the Millennium Development Goals is approaching rapidly. You, as one individual, one leader, one government, have made the commitment to the United Nations Millennium Declaration and you collectively have the power to make a difference. Renew that commitment – and make it a reality.

SECOND PLACE – SENIOR

Peadar O'Lamhna

*St. Macartan's College, Monaghan,
Ireland, Age 18*

**MDG 2 – ACHIEVE UNIVERSAL
PRIMARY EDUCATION**

Mr. President, Mr. Secretary-General, Ladies and Gentlemen,

On this day ten years ago the world was a very different place. As the political leaders were signing up to the UN Millennium Development Goals, Ireland was planning to boycott the Sydney Olympics. The most powerful man in the world today was an unknown Illinois Senator and his Secretary of State was entertaining in the White House as First Lady of the United States. The world was at peace. Ten years later, while new words may have entered our vocabulary such as Obama, You Tube, Facebook, Swine Flu, some words are still haunting us such as Acquired Immune Deficiency Syndrome, hunger, poverty and developing. We have now stained our hands with the bloodshed of two wars which are still ongoing. The threat of nuclear weapons is getting worse by the day.

However, your Excellencies, I would like to remind you of the promise you made to the 2.2 billion children of the world on 8 September 2000. You as a collective body promised that "By 2015, children everywhere, boys and girls alike, will be able to complete a full course of primary schooling".

Ten years later, however, 58 out of 86 developing world countries have still not achieved their target. I feel an election motto from the 2004 Irish general election would be suitable here: "A lot done, more to do."

While your work has seen the universal primary enrolment increase to 88 per cent there is still 12 per cent waiting for their chance to receive the gift of knowledge, an everlasting present, the gift of primary education. Did you know, Secretary-General, that nearly a billion people entered the twenty-first century unable to sign their name or read a book? That, Secretary-General, was more than the combined populations of Andorra, Australia, Austria, Belgium, Canada, Denmark, Finland, France, Germany, Greece, Iceland, Ireland, Israel, Italy, Japan, Luxembourg, Malta, Monaco, The Netherlands, New Zealand, Norway, Portugal, Slovenia, Spain, Sweden, Switzerland, the UK and the USA! While that statistic may shock your Excellencies, what is even more shocking is that two-thirds of the 855,000,000 people I mentioned were women. Action needs to be taken if the goal is to be reached by 2015 and not 2115.

There is an Irish proverb, Secretary-General, *"Tús maith, leath na hoibre"* – A good start, half the work. While we as an International body did get off to a good start with funding the Millennium Development Goals, the onset of two international wars in the Middle East has hampered efforts by this body to reach their goals. What makes it more shocking is that this peace-based body sanctioned the war in Iraq by removing its weapons inspectors to pave the way for an invasion by certain member states. The UN did this in full knowledge of the financial implications on member states in fulfilling the MDGs and funding a war in both Afghanistan and Iraq.

Less than one per cent of what the world spent every year on weapons during these wars was needed to put every child into school, and yet it didn't happen. The countries involved seemed more fascinated with the outcome of their endeavours by bombing innocent cilivians' homes and displacing millions of people instead of funding children to receive education and universal schooling.

According to 2007 statistics, $186,000 was spent on every minute of every day on the war in Iraq. If this money was spent on education it could have been used to fund 21,510,598 full four-year scholarships to public universities, 7,689,734 new public school teachers and 58,770,981 chances for children to attend "Head Start" in the United States alone. Imagine how this money could have been used in the developing world where the cost of living and wages is far less than the first world. Schools could have been built, new teachers trained and each child given the primary education that they deserve.

Mr. Secretary-General, $5 billion was spent on achieving the Millennium Development Goal regarding universal primary education in 2006. This is far from the $11 billion needed for this goal to be achieved by 2015. You as an international body must prioritise what comes first, funding weapons or funding education. Another proverb comes to mind: "Feed a man a fish he'll live for a day, teach a man to fish he'll live for a lifetime." By providing education we are opening a door for children by providing them with the key to a better society – that key being education.

We live in a world where change is the buzzword on the lips of many of its citizens. Change in politics, climate change, policy changes – the list is endless. But I put it to you, world leaders, that change is needed on your part if we are to succeed in implementing the Millennium Development Goals. We, as a global society, are tired of listening to endless pledges but seeing very little action. We are sick of the endless television advertisements which remind us on a daily basis that an Ethiopian orphan could receive schooling for as little as €14 per month. Is this not what we expected when we voted you all into office?

Instead of the millions being spent on wining and dining your government ministers and visiting dignitaries, should this money not have been spent on ensuring the MDGs were met and in particular that each child would receive a primary education, be they boy or girl, black or white or Indian or Irish?

May I remind the members of this chamber of what they or their predecessors signed up to on 10 December 1948. Article 26 of the UN Declaration of Human Rights states that "Everyone has the right to education", that the "education they receive shall be free, at least in the elementary and fundamental stages and that this elementary education shall be compulsory". The article also states: "Education shall be directed to the full development of the human personality and to the strengthening of respect for human rights and fundamental freedoms. It shall promote understanding, tolerance and friendship among all nations, racial or religious groups, and shall further the activities of the United Nations for the maintenance of peace."

The article concludes by stating that "Parents have a prior right to choose the kind of education that shall be given to their children". If by 2015, Millennium Development Goal number 2 has not been reached, the UN has failed in its mission, it has not fulfilled the promises it has laid out to help the needy of the world, and it is in contravention of its own constitution!

In order for an international crisis to be averted – and a redrafting of the UN declaration – there is a simple action that each member state can do no matter how big or small they are, no matter how wealthy or bankrupt. If the world combines together and gathers $2 from each of the 6,692,030,277 people of the world for the next five years these goals would be achieved. People don't mind paying taxes if they are to be used for helping others instead of funding corrupt political systems.

In summary, Secretary-General, I thank you for giving me this opportunity to address this fine assembly. I congratulate you on the work so far in achieving the Millennium Development Goals and I hope that I can address you once more in 2015 to congratulate you on giving every child on the planet the gift of not only primary but also secondary education. I leave you with a quote from the American psychiatrist Theodore Rubin, who when asked to describe hard work and happiness said: "Happiness does not come from doing easy work but from the afterglow of satisfaction that comes after the achievement of a difficult task that demanded our best." Fulfilling the Millennium Development Goals will demand our best but the happiness gained by them will last a lifetime.

JOINT THIRD PLACE – SENIOR

Sarah Foley

Loreto Secondary School,
Wexford, Ireland, Age 16

MDG 2 – ACHIEVE UNIVERSAL
PRIMARY EDUCATION

Mr. President, Mr. Secretary-General, Ladies and Gentlemen, it is an honour and a privilege to be here today. I stand before you all with great respect and admiration. You all have something that I and most other people would give anything for. You all have an opinion that counts for something. You all have the ability to make important decisions. You all have the power to make the world a better place. It is something you should all be very proud of.

So how did you all get here? How did all 192 of you climb your way up to the top of world leadership? Each and every one of you has a different past, a different struggle that you had to overcome in order to get to this point in your life, a different reason for getting here. Yet you all have one very important thing in common. You all had the self-belief that you could follow your dreams and become leaders and you all achieved that. Congratulations. But where did that self-belief come from? Some of you may not know, in fact you may not have even been aware that you had it. But you do and I'll tell you how you got it. It was instilled in you as you were educated.

As you learned about the countries around the world, the science of the universe, and the great works of Shakespeare and Frost you were also learning about yourself. You were learning that you too could be as a great as the people that you learned about, that you too could make a difference. You learned that the purpose of your life was to be great, and more importantly you learned that you were able to achieve that greatness. But that was not written in any book that you came across or any math problem that you solved. That was accomplished because you were educated, not because of the things you learned in school. Education instils greatness. Education promotes change. Education empowers life. It is perhaps the greatest gift you could give someone because it can never be taken away from them. It is theirs for life.

In the year 2000, 189 world leaders signed on to the Millennium Declaration seeking to end extreme World poverty by 2015. At the time there was a sense of great urgency that something had to be done. Ten years on that urgency still remains. Throughout the past ten years there has been both progress and set backs but that 2015 date is still firmly in the backs of everyone's head. There are eight goals that we want to accomplish, all vital in the task of ending poverty. But I would like to draw your attention to Goal Two, Universal Primary Education.

The target is simple. By 2015 the Millennium Development Goals want to ensure that every child in the world, whether they are boys or girls, black or white, Christian or Muslim, completes a full course of primary education. The task of ensuring that goal, however, is no mean feat.

How can you ensure that all children are receiving a proper education when there are no legal documents stating that these children even exist? How do you persuade a father to let his sons go to school when they are needed to work in order to provide for their families? How do you convince a woman dying of AIDS that her daughter should be in school instead of at home looking after her? The answer is in the question. Education. We must get people to learn. Learn that the only way out of poverty is through education.

Education ensures a better life for both the student and their families. And we are not talking about Degrees in Philosophy or a PhD in Nuclear Science. We are talking about learning how to survive. Learning about how to produce food, keep themselves free from disease and infection and, most importantly, learning about change. If we don't teach these children that there is something better out there, a future where hunger and disease are a thing of the past, then how can they be expected to achieve these things?

W.B. Yeats once said, "Education is not filling a pail but lighting a fire". These children need a chance to set the world on fire. But first they must be taught how.

We are all taught that we are born equal and perhaps that is true. At the time of their birth all babies are equal. But that doesn't last. From the moment after their birth onwards no two children on this earth are equal in the sense of them being given equal chances. Some are given food and shelter, some aren't. Some are given a loving family, some aren't. Some are given a chance to educate themselves, some aren't.

At this moment in time there are more than 100 million children who don't go to school. And should we forget about those children who have grown up? It is estimated that 872 million adults in developing countries are illiterate today. So if any of you are under the illusion all men and women are born equal then you are wrong. Some are given a chance, some aren't.

Education opens many doors to people and you will go far with it, but it will never make you any more important. In fact, if education has taught me anything it has taught me just that. I am not any more important than a child starving in the blistering African heat, or a nameless victim of the devastating Haiti earthquake or anyone sitting here in front of me. We are all just people. We all have hopes and fears, dreams and regrets. But what is different about us is our influence in the world. A small child has little influence over whether or not they will go to bed hungry. I have little influence over whether my country's government makes more cuts in social welfare, but you, you're all a different story. You all have a great influence over your countries' actions, and your neighbours' countries. You are the key to action, the key to change. It is a great responsibility and I speak on behalf of all us who have only a small voice when I say, do something now, before it's too late.

We are all too aware of the suffering that goes on in the world, whether it's plagued at us as images through the media or it's on our front door. There is no escaping from the suffering of those who have no choice but to endure utter poverty. But we must give them a way out. Give them life. Give them an education. Instead of focusing on the misery and coming up with short-term solutions that don't last, we must teach these victims how to get out of poverty for themselves. Instead of poverty being the reality, let it be something that future generations learn about in their history classes, with amazement that life was ever like that for the generations before them. I hope and I pray that that day will come very soon.

Imagine, for a moment, a world where every single person on the planet was educated. Everyone had an equal chance to achieve greatness. Think of where that could take us. Imagine the advances that could be made in science. Imagine the talent that could be discovered in the arts. Imagine the progress that could be made in the peace efforts.

In order for this progress to be made we must ensure that basic education is available to all children. These children will learn how to look after themselves and then go home and teach their parents. The message will spread quickly, trust me. Allow my generation to teach yours. I believe this is the only way forward if poverty is to be stopped in the next five years. People will never see that there is another way unless they are taught about it. Allow these children to want more from life. Education not only teaches people facts and figures, it teaches people to think for themselves, make their own decisions. It gives them a voice of their own.

The year 2015 is quickly approaching. It is no longer the far off horizon that it was ten years ago, but do not let that falter your hopes and plans to reach this goal you have set. You have all done tremendous work and I applaud your sincerely for it. But there is still much work to be done. If these people are to be are to be given any chance in life they need to be educated. You are giving them a life changing gift that will enrich their lives in ways we may never understand, because in the words of John Dewey: "Education is not preparation for life; education is life itself."

JOINT THIRD PLACE – SENIOR

Nancy Jane Carragher

Presentation Secondary School,
Thurles, Co. Tipperary, Ireland,
Age 17

MDG 1 – ERADICATE EXTREME POVERTY AND HUNGER

Mr. President, Mr. Secretary-General, Ladies and Gentlemen, I'm here today to speak to you on one of the Millennium Development Goals. I have chosen to speak about the eradication of extreme poverty and hunger. I believe that this issue is central to all others, and urgently needs addressing.

In the Paris declaration on aid effectiveness the ministers of many countries resolved to take "far-reaching and measurable actions to reform the ways we deliver and manage aid". Since then they have continuously reiterated this heart-warming promise. And yet, according to the World Bank, as many as 40 nations are either off-track or seriously off-track in meeting these targets.

It was estimated by the United Nations MDG report 2009 that some 55-90 million more people will live in extreme poverty than had been projected before the economic and financial crisis. That is frankly disheartening.

Globally, the number of hungry people rose from 842 million in 1990-92 to 1.02 billion people in 2009. That, Ladies and Gentlemen, is simply ridiculous. A promise once made, must be kept, and that applies even more so to our situation, because when 1.02 billion people do not have enough to eat, a promise is a lifeline.

We are not just obliged to keep that promise. We're not just bound to that promise. If the only thing we do right in our entire lives is saving those starving men, women and children's lives, then that would be more than enough. We are responsible for every single death that occurs when our aid does not work. We have to keep these promises, these oaths that many depend on, that many cling to for hope. We have to do our utmost best; there is simply no other option.

According to the UN AIDS global report on the AIDS epidemic, in Sub-Saharan Africa alone, AIDS has orphaned over 12 million children. Every six seconds a child dies of hunger and related causes according to a recent FAO report. Unfortunately, I could go on and on and on. But that would just be adding to the delay and rhetoric. How many times does one need to resolve to end world poverty and hunger before the action begins? When are we going to see some real action in reaching our targets and in perfecting aid effectiveness? When will we see this much-needed change? Tomorrow? Next week? In a few months? In five years? And will it actually ever happen?

At the world food summit on food security, all states and governments declared that they agreed to undertake all necessary actions required on every level to halt immediately the increase in – and to sufficiently reduce – the number of people suffering from hunger, malnutrition and food insecurity. They committed to take action towards sustainably eradicating hunger at the earliest possible date! Well, Ladies and Gentlemen, I'd like to know when is the earliest possible date? Because the mothers of the children dying every six seconds, the 1.02 billion starving people and the entire world is wondering if not now, then when? The earliest possible date, when undertaking every single necessary action, is certainly not in five years' time, because by that time, Ladies and Gentlemen, over 26 million children will have died due to hunger-related causes alone.

As the President of the World Bank said: "Progress has been made. But we have to move faster. We know what needs to be done. With the Paris declaration we have the blueprint to do it." What's left to do is to take action. We have promised, we have sworn, we have analysed, monitored, increased staff and budgets, and now, now we have to implement all that hard work. Now, Ladies and Gentlemen, or never.

I know we've hit an economic crisis. I know times are tough! But time isn't so tough that a lack of vitamin A will kill us. That's the difference between us and one million infants per year. We do not lack something as basic as vitamin A. They do. We have cars, homes, jobs and education. We, Ladies and Gentlemen, have lives and most importantly human dignity.

Perhaps some think that a cut in their paychecks is devastating; perhaps some think longingly of the days when they didn't have to budget their weekly shopping and expenses. But that is nothing compared to the extreme and horrific poverty which is prevalent in too many countries in this world today. Their poverty is on us. Those people living on under $1.25 a day, their miserable lives are on us. That's our problem and we have to fix it. As Kofi Annan once said, "suffering anywhere concerns people everywhere". So we bravely committed to help these people, these strangers who we don't know; we have given them a promise, so let's keep it. We only have five years left to deliver on this pledge, this guarantee. So what are we going to do?

For one we can seriously look into aid effectiveness. Spending millions on development of hospitals and schools will do nothing to sustainably help the receiving population if they are suffering from famine or drought or are unable to grow crops on their land due to climate change. It may look good, but that aid does not work. We must learn to embrace these impoverished countries and include them in important discussions on their own countries' well-being, instead of patronisingly presuming we know best.

And what about the ice-resistant motorway (which was costly to construct) in the Sahara desert? Was that a valuable usage of aid money? I think not!

Every cent matters and we must use each cent effectively to fully harness the potential of aid in achieving lasting results, in eradicating world poverty and hunger. Ladies and Gentlemen, if we are making progress then it is not enough and it won't be enough until this entire world is devoid of any hungry or impoverished peoples.

In the Accra talks it was decided that to accelerate progress country ownership, building more effective and inclusive partnerships and achieving development results and openly accounting for them were key. But it seems somebody forgot to mention human rights, and by not focusing on this central issue aid is immediately doomed to hit the wrong targets, and becomes completely ineffective.

Building more effective and inclusive partnerships are stated as part of our efforts, and defined as key in the situation. Yet this has been widely ignored and misinterpreted. It does not mean that donors can use aid to gain footing in the recipient countries, or that the partnerships somehow signal a business deal, where both sides give and take. Inclusive partnerships suggest that while allocating aid to different sectors and making decisions for the starving masses all over the world, you should not just consult but fully include the recipients in the decision making process.

What is the point, Ladies and Gentlemen, of giving out all this aid just to see it dwindle away? Didn't your mothers ever tell you that money doesn't grow on trees? It's not something to be thrown with a sympathetic smile at developing countries. Every cent that is ineffectively spent is a complete and utter waste.

If it were a business deal, and you weren't just giving away money "because you can", you can guarantee any wastage wouldn't be tolerated. You'd want the best for your money, because you're not just giving it away, your investing it, and you can feel the benefits of it yourself in your fatter paycheck. But aid is investing too; it's just investing in lives of others. It's saying you do care, and ineffective aid is saying you want to look like you care, but you don't really. Maybe because we don't see the impact or rather lack of impact ineffective aid has we don't care so much. If a child was dying every six seconds in the developed countries of this world, something would be done about it, not at the earliest possible date, a vague and annoying time restriction; no, something would be done about it now. Today, not tomorrow.

I understand the magnitude of the problems today do not have a simple solution that would be implemented in a day. But the truth is, if that poverty was visible to us day in day out, we would use every single available resource, and truly take every necessary action to solve the problem. We have discussed this and debated that, we have tried this and tested that; enough of the rhetoric and the analysis, in the words of the UN campaign, let's stand up and take action.

Ladies and Gentlemen, Nelson Mandela once said: "Sometimes it falls upon a generation to be great. You can be that generation." It has fallen upon this generation and many before it to fix world poverty and hunger. Let's succeed, Ladies and Gentlemen, let's take action, let's solve this problem and keep our promises, and let's do it now.

SHORTLIST – SENIOR

Naoise Dolan

High School, Rathgar, Dublin, Ireland, Age 17

MDG 1 – ERADICATE EXTREME POVERTY AND HUNGER

Mr. President, Mr. Secretary-General, Ladies and Gentlemen,

It's easy to lose sight of the urgency. When you have 15 years to do something, you feel a tremendous sense of control. This is doable. This will change the world. This will heal all wounds, join all hands. We will look each other in the eyes and smile freely, knowing that we are equal. We will be liberated – the developing countries from poverty, the developed ones from guilt. And we will do something, day by day, piece by piece, and every brick laid will be one brick closer to a finished wall. We can do this. That sort of thing.

The thing is, you don't go down in history for having the ability to do something. Your name won't appear in newspapers with the headline: "Joe Blogs has made a plan to end world hunger." We remember those who did, not those who considered doing. Maybe you like this system of values, maybe you don't. Regardless, it's the one that will judge you and the countries you represent if you don't deliver as promised.

You have had ten years to deliberate. In a flurry of ambition, fit for the fight, you used the first few to implement – to act, even. However, in the past five, not only have you stopped cycling up the hill, you've begun to let the bike fall backwards. Soon you'll be at the bottom all over again. Your time will have run out.

Your seconds are ticking away. So are theirs.

Please understand that I don't mean to be rude any more than an alarm clock does. When it's early in the morning and you're settled nicely in your bed, the ringing seems like a spiteful intrusion, but you must realise that its set of wheels and cogs that turn because you told them to. It rings loudly because that's what you need. You need to pull off the duvet and rise. There's no sense in escaping from the escapements – you've set the clock, and now it's blaring loud and clear.

Your countries promised to end hunger. Not to stall hunger; not to temporarily fill stomachs and then watch them grow vacant again. To end it. The deadline is approaching. There is more time behind you than there is remaining. I assure you that hunger does not wait. It doesn't take a wavering economy into account. It doesn't check the size of your national deficit before taking lives. Good times or bad times, people are starving.

Forget about me, and forget about history. You won't have to answer to us if you'll only answer to them. Answer to the pinched, perishing people with eyes gaping widely out of their heads and their stomachs puffing out in a cruel pastiche of fullness. Tell them why, in this age of technology, you cannot find the food to feed them. Tell them what they're going hungry for. You owe them that much. They won't be here forever, these withering souls; right now they're fading, and soon they'll have faded. If they cannot eat, they cannot speak. You are losing their stories. Their voices are evaporating. They have so much to contribute to this world of ours, and you're squandering it.

I know that it's not customary to use an accusatory tone when you're begging. There's a reason that homeless people don't hold up signs saying, "Your government has failed me; the least you can do is buy me a sandwich". It makes people uncomfortable. They feel attacked. The traditional approach is to accentuate the positive. Don't tell people that not helping is wrong; instead, tell them that helping is right. Plead with them, and keep all hints of bitterness, all traces of blame, out of your voice.

110

I refuse to condescend to you in such a fashion. You don't need empty, patronising flattery. You need the resonating rattle of an alarm clock at six in the morning, clear, cold and just. That's the worst thing about the alarm clock – it's always right. It goes off on the dot. There's no arguing with that sort of reason. It's too simple to find a flaw.

I present you with that variety of reasoning. You promised to do something, and now you must do it.

If excuses could feed mouths, we'd have no one going to bed hungry. If procrastination could stop the hunger pangs, the air would be untainted with the screams of agony. If skewed priorities could put roofs over heads, there'd be shelter for everyone.

And if hope could unshackle us, we'd all be free from poverty.

Hope. It's the most and least inspiring thing about this goal. It elevates me to think how much you can do; it depresses me that you don't do it. You are all good people who have a desire to help mankind. You and your countries are brimming with potential. You have the will and the resources to do something about world hunger. I firmly believe that if one man were starving, you'd help him. If three were, you'd persuade the people sitting on either side of you to contribute. If dozens were, this entire room would stand up and do something.

Millions are, but there are millions of people on your side. This isn't a flight of fancy. Asking you to end world hunger and reduce poverty is, essentially, nothing but the one starving man principle taken to its logical extreme. The ratios are hardly threatening: 18 million a year die of poverty-related causes, but how many more millions could you enlist to help them? You have powerful flags, powerful governments, powerful people, all happily at your command. They're ready and willing. Many of them are suffering from charity fatigue, but they'll still gladly do their duty.

They need to understand this, and so do you. What you're doing isn't charity. It's breathtaking, it's staggering, it's almost terrifying in its exaltation. But it isn't charity. There is far more to this goal than doing something nice and getting a pat on the back. For the first time in history, you can face up to your responsibilities. The onus is upon you, and by accepting it, you are doing what your ancestors failed to. We could argue for hours about imperialism and multinational corporations, but that's not what I mean when I say that you owe it to these people. Let's leave your predecessors and your peers behind and deal with the most recent and relevant fact of all: your countries promised to do this.

Five years may seem like an age to get something done, but you must start somewhere. Every moment makes a difference. Don't wait for the financial crisis to end; you'll have lost too many by then. Don't wait until the year is out and you've caught up a bit on your budget deficits; you'll still have lost too many lives. Don't even wait until tomorrow, because another 50,000 will have passed away needlessly by then, and I hope I'm not alone in thinking that 50,000 entirely preventable deaths are 50,000 too many.

You keep the principles of the United Nations ingrained in our hearts and minds. When we seek to define your work, we don't look to the past, but rather to the present, and every day we see these tenets of unity in action. You have my utmost regard. There's only one thing more intimidating than speaking to you, and that's criticising you. I make this speech now so that in five years the world in its entirety will be able to thank you sincerely and unconditionally. You are the General Assembly, you need not flinch. It's beneath you to claim to stand for co-operation to an extent, equality within reason, justice for all except ... I'm not going to finish that sentence. You are not an organisation that makes exceptions, and that's why we all look to you.

You have done remarkable things to earn our respect, and now you need to do remarkable things to keep it. You said that you would rise at six in the morning. Gentle prodding hasn't woken you; the birds have been singing, the light streaming in through the filter of your curtains, to no avail. The alarms are ringing because they have to. They'll keep going, these alarms, through walls, through buildings, echoing across borders. They will be understood in every language. If they need to, they'll burst your eardrums.

They won't, though, because it won't take that much. You are honest, upstanding people representing countries that are proud of you, and you will do what you have promised to do.

I have faith in you. We all do. Show us that we were right to trust you. Thank you so much for your time.

SHORTLIST – SENIOR

Paul Kelly

Wesley College, Dublin, Ireland, Age 18

MDG 8 – DEVELOP A GLOBAL PARTNERSHIP FOR DEVELOPMENT

Mr. President, Mr. Secretary-General, Ladies and Gentlemen,

I stand before you today to tell you that much has been accomplished in our struggle to develop a global partnership for development. The world is now more interdependent than it has ever been before. Telecommunications has revolutionised this planet as mobile phone usage and broadband access increase everyday. These Millennium Development Goals are no longer lofty, idealistic ambitions: They are attainable, reachable and more necessary than ever before. Slowly, ever so slowly, we are hacking away at the problems of exploitation, unfair trading and neo-colonialism which are plaguing our world.

Together we are struggling for a brighter future. Together we are finally deciding that the cruelties of this world must be stopped and that there is only one time when this can be accomplished. That time is now.

Esteemed heads of state, we have struggled to work interdependently since the dawn of time. Since the dawn of time we have looked upon other peoples as mere tools towards our own progress: how their crops could feed us; how their riches could clothe us. It was with this ignorance, ladies and gentlemen, that the unfair trade practices of this world were laid down. It is this ignorance which, for too long, has held back the people of this world. It is this ignorance that is still forcing 40 per cent of the world's population to live on less than 5 per cent of the world's wealth.

My friends, this goal is made up of six parts. Five of these six parts are directly linked back to trade. If we had fairer trade practices this goal would not have to exist, indeed none of the Millennium Development Goals would have to exist. Fairer trade practices would mean that every farmer, North and South, would receive a fair price for their produce. The prices of basic commodities would no longer fluctuate and with this consistency would come progress. Nations could plan their economies with increasing statistical awareness and soon hunger and poverty would be eradicated as jobs are created in the global growth centres of every economy. Where now 30 per cent of the world are without jobs, full employment would follow. With fairer trade practices, technology could be shared easily without tied debt and cruel trading prices holding it back. Prices for this new technology would be index-marked to the prices of these basic commodities resulting in less economically developed countries finally being able to industrialise as they gain fair prices for their produce. Industry would flourish on the back of agricultural production and there would never again be a want for the basic necessities of life. Poverty would be eradicated.

The goal is clear; the benefits of a global partnership for development are obvious. All that is left to be done is to grasp that goal. The time is now.

As the benefits of fairer trade practices seep into all layers of society the nations of the world will prosper. Where 121 million children now have no access to education, this number will be halved. Why? Simply because every government will not only see the benefits of educated workers for the growth sectors of tomorrow, they will have the capital to produce these workers too. But this global increase in education can only occur on the back of fairer trade practices. It can only occur when multinational corporations begin to think ethically as well as economically. It can only occur when an end is put to the profit flight which dominates so many of these corporation's polices. This profit flight is just one example of the unfair trading which is crushing the economies of so many nations, pushing them to the edge that only a branch plant economy can balance on.

Even as education prospers, so too will the health sector. Just as more and more engineers emerge from the universities of the world so too will more and more doctors. And these doctors will strive to create better and more effective treatments; will strive to, at last, once and for all, end the scourge of HIV/AIDS across the world. Where now 33.4 million live with this deadly disease, there will be none. In this way too, the mothers and children of the world will never again lack basic care. The maternal mortality ratio will plunge. As education increases the children of the new millennium will grow into a world of prosperity and peace unhindered by the ignorance of gender discrimination.

And even as the new industries of this world rise, so too will the old industries fall, and, in its turn, so will our dependence on fossil fuels. New technology will slow and halt the ever present threat of global warming upon this world. Soon the advantages of sustainable forestry will become economically more viable than deforestation ever could be. Esteemed heads of state, we stand upon the threshold of a new world. All we need now do is cross that threshold. The time is now.

My friends, I am conscious always of the difficulties this goal poses. But I stand before you today to tell you that these difficulties are not insurmountable. Progress is already being made: debt is decreasing, telecommunications technology is expanding and the markets of the world are slowly being opened to even the least developed countries. These successes are significant but they are as nothing compared to what must follow.

Agricultural subsidies in the rich countries of this world continue to hinder the development of intensive agricultural production in dozens of other nations. Esteemed heads of state, we are in need of a Green Revolution, not just in any one nation, but globally. This Green Revolution is essential to combat poverty and hunger everywhere, but it can only come about if these unfair trade practices are removed. Removing these subsidies and tariff barriers will not be easy. Jobs will be lost, wages in agricultural employment will fall and rural to urban migration will rise rapidly. Where now the Common Agricultural Policy and other unfair trade practices stem the flow, an explosion will follow.

These trade practices provide a fair living for farmers in rich, developed, countries but, by placing protective tariff barriers on the EU, they are crushing production in poorer countries. The removal of these trade practices will cost these rich nations dearly but they must be removed in order to allow the poor of this world to live. These are burdens that the rich must shoulder. These are burdens which, for too long, the poor of this world have been forced to shoulder. This cannot continue. We cannot break the shackles of hardship and poverty through words alone. All the aid of this world is for naught if we do not breathe upon this world a new spirit of fair trade. A spirit that deals with the needs of the least developed countries of this world, a spirit that will value people over profit. A spirit that we have within us, my friends, all we do must do is release it upon the markets of this world. The time is now.

Esteemed heads of state, your fellow man is calling out to you for help. How could we ever ignore him? Already we are seeing the effects of global warming on those in the most need: crops are failing, animals are dying and desertification is spreading. These effects are caused by the rich, industrialised peoples of this world and we must work together to slow and halt them. We must work together to end trade discrimination and put the development of the least developed as our number one priority. We must work together to develop each country's infrastructure so they can meet the tide of the new millennium and the problems of the growing financial crisis.

Esteemed leaders, we are at a pivotal point in the history of this planet. For the first time in human history we, at last, have the opportunity to end the spread of hunger, poverty and disease. We, at last, have the opportunity to provide education to all. We, at last, have the opportunity to heal the wounds inflicted on the poorest countries of this world – a healing which can only begin through the implementation of fairer trade practices. This goal will not be easy: It will cost hundreds of jobs and livelihoods in the developed countries of this world. But it is a goal that can and must be achieved to save millions of lives in developing countries.

Through the building of a global partnership for development we can stride into the future with our heads held high. Our children will grow into a world where economic oppression is but a distant memory – because we ended it. They will grow into a world of prosperity. They will grow into a world where war no longer exists, because economic strife has disappeared. Ladies and gentleman, we have the resources, ability and will to accomplish this. We must act.

The time is now.

SHORTLIST – SENIOR

Lucy Jones

Loreto College, Fermoy, Co. Cork,
Ireland, Age 17

MDG 2 – ACHIEVE UNIVERSAL PRIMARY EDUCATION

Mr. President, Mr. Secretary-General, Ladies and Gentlemen, why is it that I have the honour of addressing you tonight? Is it because my oratory skills rival those of Voltaire? Is it because I am as great a writer as Shakespeare himself? Or is it because there is no one else who possesses such a capable mind as myself? No, it is none of these things. I am neither a great writer nor speaker, nor have I the highest I.Q. I am but a mere school girl, but aha, herein lies the reason I stand before you tonight. I unlike millions of others am a schoolgirl. I have been privileged enough to be taught to put these words to paper. I have been granted a basic human right, my right to education.

The right to education has been established as a basic human right since 1952 yet more than half a decade later millions of children are still being denied the most basic education – a primary school education. When we deny a child the rudimentary tools – such as teachers and classrooms – to educate itself we deny it a future, and as we continue to do so, to the children of developing countries we doom these countries as well. It is no surprise that an educated population is directly linked to economic growth and prosperity. The performance of any country can be assessed by the literacy rate of that country. The countries which have the highest number of educated people – the United States, Germany, the United Kingdom – are the most advanced states in the world. One glance at the table of global literacy rates says it all with countries such as Mali, Niger and Chad trailing behind. Education cannot be underestimated. Throughout history it can be seen that well-educated citizens are crucial to the survival of a democratic society, a peaceful society, a society in which citizens enjoy a reasonable standard of living. Education is the only sustainable end to world poverty and path to peace and security.

Education is not only an important goal in itself but it is also indispensable in the realisation of many others, such as gender equality, maternal and child health and the combat of HIV/AIDS and other diseases. By ensuring that children everywhere, boys and girls alike, will be able to complete a full course of primary schooling we go a long way in promoting gender equality. As it stands today, two-thirds of children denied primary education are girls and 75 per cent of the world's 876 million illiterate adults are women. Ladies and gentlemen, it is impossible to achieve gender equality without universal education. Men and women simply cannot stand on equal footing without equal knowledge. It has also been shown that young people who have completed primary education are less than half as likely to contract HIV as those missing an education. Universal primary education would prevent 700,000 cases of HIV each year – about 30 per cent of all new infections in young people.

Better education also results in better health for mothers and children because of better access to crucial information and health care. In Ethiopia, women with at least some education are 260 per cent more likely to receive antenatal care than women with no education. In essence, being educated has significant health advantages for both adults and children in the developing world. The importance of education for the completion of all the Millennium Development Goals by 2015 cannot be overestimated. As William Allin once said: "Education is not the answer to the question. Education is the means to the answer to all questions."

Ladies and gentlemen, every human being should have an opportunity to make a better life for themselves. What we do to the children of developing countries by not providing them with the most basic education – a primary school education – is unspeakable. With no education there is little employment and millions of children must resort to prostitution, crime or labour in the agricultural sector, mining and gold washing, or domestic servants in urban areas. By providing a child with a primary school education we are indirectly giving it the gift of childhood. A child in school is a child – for at least a portion of the day – off the streets, out of the picking fields, away from the misery that desolate poverty causes. What you and your countries give when you provide a child with primary school education cannot solely be measured in literacy rates or GNP figures.

William Kirwan once said that "education changes the lives of the people who will change the world". We have already established that it is my education which has granted me the honour of addressing you today, but how many of you would be sitting here before me today if your abilities were not nurtured by an excellent education? We have been privileged and now we must work with expedience to achieve goal two of the Millennium Development Goals: Universal Primary School Education. Socrates said: "The only good is knowledge and the only evil is ignorance."

SHORTLIST – SENIOR

Annie Clarke

Bailieboro Community School, Co, Cavan, Ireland, Age 17

MDG 4 – REDUCE CHILD MORTALITY

Good afternoon, Mr. President, Mr. Secretary-General, Ladies and Gentlemen, Distinguished Guests. My name is Jayvyn – it means light spirit – and I was from Sub-Saharan Africa. But I address you now from beyond the grave. I died three years ago, at the age of five, from a combination of malaria and starvation. It was very painful, but I am not here to talk about me. I'm here to talk about the Millennium Goals, and one in particular.

The issue of child mortality is, clearly, something close to my heart, and a serious problem that is affecting more and more people every day, particularly in underdeveloped countries. In Sub-Saharan Africa, child mortality rates are running at an average of 172 deaths per 1,000 children, compared with 9 per 1,000 in developed regions. Every year, more than 10 million children die of curable disease – that's 30,000 per day. Well over 1,200 children in this world die every hour from preventable causes.

But these are just figures and facts, just cold numbers. They cannot express to you the pain that each individual child feels as he or she takes their last breath, or the anguish that a family member goes through as they lose their loved one. They cannot explain to you the struggle I went through to survive, or the broken, hurt defeat with which I surrendered to death. But the fact still stands that one out of every ten children dies before the age of five in low income countries. You hear all the time about children dying in vast numbers – perhaps so much so that you are desensitized to it? It can seem like just another figure, not a person's life. But that little person is someone's daughter, someone's son, cousin, friend or grandchild, somebody's treasure. That little person is also gone. The reality of these dying children is much crueller, much harsher than any simple statistics can convey – you would have to witness it firsthand, or go through it yourself, to understand how great a burden the loss of a child is.

Some of the main causes of child mortality are diseases such as HIV/AIDS or malaria, starvation, under-resourced health services, acute respiratory infections, war ... the list goes on. Many of these things can be so easily resolved, which is where the Millennium Goal comes into play. However, at the moment, they are not being resolved. If they were, would there still be more than 600,000 new cases of HIV in children every year? I want you to know that this aim, the reduction of under-five child mortality by two thirds, is not only admirable in theory, it is achievable. It can be done. You, the powerful people of our planet, have the resources to help us- and it is so important that you do. Children are the world's greatest hope. They are innocence and compassion and love. They are, for the most part, untouched by the anger and lies of older generations, and their simple caring hearts are what will guide us through to better times. Without children, there would be no hope. A little more hope fades with every little boy or girl that perishes.

Despite all the hardships my fellow youth and I faced, and despite all the despair, death and destruction that occurs every day, there is so much more beauty in the world than ugliness. And you, the most influential people among us, have much of it at your fingertips. You have so much of it that perhaps you take it for granted sometimes and forget how blessed you are. But the young children of my nation cannot forget. Cannot forget their empty stomachs, their hopelessness, helplessness, or the distinct lack of beauty that surrounds them. They are dying, and with them – with us – dies potential; with us dies the future.

Imagine the sound of a child laughing. There is no lighter, happier sound in the entire universe, than that of a child's laughter. They are so carefree and joyful when they laugh, and they laugh with their whole hearts, with such faith in the inherent goodness of the world. They laugh even before they can talk. Now compare this with the ragged screams of a harmed toddler, a confused and tormented baby. It is enough to make your heart break. Children should never have to produce such a cry as this one, but unfortunately, too many young ones learn this before they even know how to laugh. Young kids are the best of us, the most wonderful citizens of society, and the least deserving, certainly, of the horrors to which many of them are subjected.

While the Millennium Goal is mostly on track in the north of Africa – and that is fantastic – there has been basically no change to the death rates in other regions. It is the responsibility of a big brother to look after his little sister, and in much the same way, it is the responsibility of the strong and powerful to take care of the weak and vulnerable. You, our distinguished guests, represent the strong and powerful, and the children of my country are the weak and vulnerable. They need to be looked after-they need to be saved. They need to know beauty, the kind that you understand, the kind I never had. Security, safety, shelter ... all are forms of such simple, striking beauty that the children I left behind are not familiar with.

My pain was intensely real; my suffering immense. I felt it acutely every moment of my life. But I was only one child out of the thousands and millions who continue to feel this sharp, real agony every day. Multiply my simple burdens by two million and you have the number of children who were killed in a single war. Multiply my trauma by hundreds of thousands and you get the number of children that are dying from illnesses that could easily be treated. We are the unheard voices, the lost generation whose

numbers are dwindling every day. Mine was the cry of an ago-
nised nation; my voice went unheard. I ask you to hear us now.

I said before that hope is fading, but there is good news. Hope
is not dead yet. There is still time, and still a chance, still so many
children that can be saved. To cure malaria requires only between
$.08 and $5.30. That is the amount of the loose change in your
pocket, money that you would throw away. With it, someone's
life could be saved. To treat AIDS costs simply $30 per year for
every person infected. I know the world banks are currently facing troubling days, but surely health, in particular the health of
the future, is worth investing in? Surely people are worth the bet,
especially people who have not yet had the chance to discover the
world and their places within it?

I see much more now than I ever did when on earth; now I can
see everything. I see the sufferings and joys of all people, I see the
reasons behind things; I see my family doing their best to survive,
my new baby sister who will never know me. I understand why I
had to die and miss all the things I did. But I, along with countless
others, would so dearly love if the youth of my nation – my brothers and sisters – could face a better, brighter future, and I *know* it
is possible. Perhaps it is my childish idealism, but I have faith in
this goal, and confidence in your ability to carry it out. I ask you,
in the voice of a small child, but more importantly, in the voice of
a human being who was denied the most precious gift there is, to
give the children of my country the opportunity to fly. Please give
them some of the simple beauty they do not as of now have: the
beauty of dreams, and the gift of hope, the gift of life.

Thank you for listening.

SHORTLIST – SENIOR

Maria McWalter

Mount St. Michael Secondary School,
Claremorris, Co. Mayo, Ireland, Age 16

MDG 1 – ERADICATE EXTREME POVERTY AND HUNGER

Good evening Mr. President, Mr. Secretary-General, Ladies and Gentlemen, World Leaders and the International Press.

I am honoured to be here this evening and that I get the opportunity to speak to such influential world leaders. We are all here tonight for one very important reason: the Millennium Development Goals. Ten short years ago, the UN embarked into the new millennium by devising eight unique goals which would aim to finally address the unacceptable divide between the rich and poor people of this world. The first and in my opinion the most significant goal was the ambitious aim to put an end to extreme poverty and hunger in the developing world. It stated that by the year 2015, the proportion of people living on $1.00 a day would have halved and that the number of people suffering from hunger would have also halved. Have these goals been achieved yet? No, but whether they are achieved by 2015 or not is up to each and every one you here tonight. By the time I will have finished here this evening, I am confident that I will have shown you how the UN can address issues that are threatening the success of the MDGs. I am also confident that I will have shown all of you a new perspective on how these vital goals can be achieved in this ever changing world.

There are many unfair contradictions in our world today. For example, there are nearly a billion people in Africa and Asia who live on less than $1.00 a day. Can you imagine trying to live on $1.00 a day? Or even trying to provide for your family with this meagre amount? Here in the developed world, the price of a McDonald's hamburger or a chocolate bar is the equivalent of what a person in the developing world has to survive on every day. REM once sang that "everybody hurts sometimes". But they should've mentioned how one billion people suffer every day of their lives from hunger and will suffer indefinitely if firm action isn't taken. Millions of us here in the developed world still haven't accepted this injustice. Last year, the world produced enough food to feed eight billion people yet ten million children died of hunger. Fair? I don't think so. If we used a fraction of what is spent on military weapons ($700 billion in 1998) then extreme poverty and hunger would not be such a big problem. The UN's war against poverty and hunger is being threatened by the greediness of the world's banks. For every $1.00 given as aid to Africa, $25.00 is given back as debt repayment. How can Africa ever begin to thrive if they are being crippled by debt?

Answer me this: for how long can you abstain from food and clean water? A few hours or maybe even a day. Can you imagine never having proper access to these basic essentials? Can you imagine trying to compete with your neighbours just so you can salvage whatever remains of food you can find at the bottom of a rubbish bin? For those of us lucky enough, it is nearly unimaginable that millions of people experience this nightmare on a daily basis.

According to UNICEF, 25,000 die every day due to poverty and they "die quietly in some of the poorest villages on Earth, far removed from the scrutiny and the conscience of the world". But what is poverty? Is it not being able to afford that new car or holiday that you always wanted? Or even not being able to keep up your mortgage repayments? For a lot of us here in the developed

126

world we have no idea of what poverty is really like. For anybody to discover the true extent of poverty they only have to ask the person living on the street. Poverty is not simply having enough money; it is a lifestyle that millions in Africa and Asia experience through no fault of their own. People living in poverty do not know where their next meal is going to come from or if they will receive medical treatment when they need it the most. Living in poverty is a frightening and uncertain existence that no one deserves to experience in this day and age.

Hunger and poverty have more repercussions than you may know. Malnourished children may be too weak to attend school as they are more prone to illnesses. For those children who are fortunate enough to attend school, their education is at risk due to their limited food intake. Absenteeism may eventually lead to that child leaving school prematurely which causes their plight to continue for the rest of their short life.

Solving world hunger can be achieved if certain issues are addressed. In Sub-Saharan Africa, the economic downturn has plunged them deeper into turmoil than ever. It is worrying to know that the Sub-Sahara has actually digressed since the MDGs have been established. If money is used to give Sub-Saharan children three meals a day, then it will be money well spent. I'm asking you world leaders to encourage everyone you can to support NGOs such as Concern by donating money. The immense support that the NGOs have gotten in recent years have resulted in the improvement of millions of peoples lives. I am asking you to give more money to these worthwhile charities so more deaths in Africa can be prevented. As the leader of Irish NGOs said at a Roundtable Policy meeting on March 9th this year, "solving hunger is not a practical issue but a political one". It is up to all of you world leaders here tonight to strengthen social networks in Africa so social issues can be dealt with once and for all. We do not have another fifteen years to try to make things right. This is our only

127

opportunity to make historical changes, because the stark reality is that millions of lives are at stake if swift action isn't taken.

Poverty and hunger is still rife in Africa for many reasons and lack of family planning is one of them. Young girls, some of whom are younger than sixteen, are being forced with bringing up a child because they were never informed about contraception. If social initiatives are established to tackle this issue then young people can decide when they settle down to raise a family. Also, if contraception is made more widely available in Africa then families will have fewer mouths to feed.

Solving hunger in Africa can be achieved if Africa is allowed to become self-sufficient. I believe that the barren lands of Africa may one day provide people with food to eat. This is not an unattainable dream. If the dry lands of California can be irrigated then so can Africa's lands. Irrigation schemes are expensive but if fertile lands are the reward, then it will be a fair price to pay.

In the year 2000, the world was a much different place. The Twin Towers still stood majestically over New York City. And we lived in a world where today's technologies hadn't even been thought of yet. There's no denying that our society has changed dramatically, but why haven't the MDGs adapted to these changes?

The MDGs are unique for two reasons. Firstly, never has there been such an initiative which has captured the imaginations of so many people. Secondly, never before has anybody attempted to abolish the injustices which plague the developing world. The MDGs are unique and cannot be attempted over such a long-term period again. I believe that more awareness needs to be created about the MDGs. People can only support this worthy cause if they know what it aims to achieve. In this war against poverty, we need more troops to help end the plight of hunger.

I hope I have shown all of you a renewed insight into how the MDGs can be improved. To reiterate on my previous statement, we do not have another fifteen years to improve conditions in the developing world. The time for improvements is now because if the MDG's targets aren't met then it will cause millions of more deaths in Africa. I personally do not want this on our conscience. This is our one chance for change. From Nigeria to New Delhi, it is not too late for the resilient people who are living their lives the only way they know how to. My message to them is to hold on. It would be tragic if the progress that has been made so far is over-shadowed by the prospect of failure to meet the all important tar-gets. May the inspiring vision of a world free from hunger moti-vate you to address this injustice.

Thank you and goodnight.

SHORTLIST – SENIOR

Jennifer Kinsella

Colaiste Ide, Dingle, Co. Kerry, Ireland, Age 16

MDG 1 – ERADICATE EXTREME POVERTY AND HUNGER

John Donne once said: "Every man's death diminishes me, for I am involved in mankind."

Mr. President, Mr. Secretary-General, Ladies and Gentlemen, what would John Donne say if he saw the poverty in our world today? He would ask us, "Who are we?" "What are our values?" "Do we have any?" He might say that no mission is a mission im-possible. We must renew our sense of optimism. People here to-day – man has explored outer space! Neil Armstrong proved crit-ics wrong when he landed on the moon. People said it would never be done, to give up. Yet here we are, years later, wondering how could we have been so wrong.

Ladies and gentlemen, it is no longer crazy to suggest we can eradicate hunger and poverty in the next five years. It is no longer unthinkable to imagine a world where a child does not die every six seconds from hunger. This isn't hope, or even just faith, it is scientific fact. It is a goal within sight. The numbers you read in newspapers and leaflets may just be mind-numbing statistics to you and me, but behind these figures is another human being's brother, sister, Mam or Dad. Your Republic of Conscience is pleading with you to help others, to save a life. It is so tantalisingly within our reach.

We need to stop this two-steps-forward one-step-back tango we have been dancing for years and start marching forward. Lack of action has been a main cause of poverty, along with climate change and globalisation. The economic meltdown of 2008 showed how tightly the world's various economies are bound together; when the investors began to invest in resources like oil, gold and food, this lead to hunger on a never before seen scale. We must buy Fairtrade products – 75 per cent of the world's poor work in agriculture; they cannot compete with multinational corporations. However, we must not dwell on past mistakes. We need to focus our attention and accelerate the process, to achieve our target goals.

So then, what do we begin with? What way is the best way to wipe out starvation and penury? What should we invest our time in? My answer? Microfinance. Microfinance is described as enabling the poor to free themselves. This organisation gives loans, business training, mentorship and other services to small business owners who are struggling to survive. The group works in developing places in Africa, Asia, Latin America and Eastern Europe offering financial support.

For example, I recently read an article where a lady, mother of six, received $100 as she was struggling to provide an income with which to support her family. The woman, living in Calcutta, bought a new sewing machine to expand her alterations business.

The woman can now afford to educate her children (they will not be included amongst the billion other people who cannot sign their names). Her children will not be one of the 2.6 billion who do not have adequate sanitation. It has given this woman hope, belief and a happier life.

As we can imagine, the woman's spirit rose like a phoenix rising from its ashes. The best part of microfinance is that when the woman repaid her $100, this money was given to another business owner living in poverty. Our world is counting on us. It is clear we cannot save every life, but the people we can save we must. Microfinance is the way forward; it is a fool-proof way of diminishing poverty. I urge you to support this group in its attempt to stop ten million people dying this year from hunger-related deaths. Talking is not enough, we must act together.

We cannot keep offering excuses as to why we have not donated money, or why we have not supported NGOs. We must offer solutions. As taxpayers, we must allow our leaders to invest money in mosquito nets or medicine to use against the spread of infection, things that only cost pennies. We must work with our leaders and together we will combat poverty and hunger. Instead of throwing away money on trips to foreign countries and buying flash new cars, the government needs to work together with the developing countries and decide on strategies in which to keep our promises. If we don't, one million people will die this year from malaria, a preventable illness – how mad is that? With just €40 a poor family in Rwanda can buy hens to provide food for themselves and sell the eggs at their local market for a profit. It may be a small sum of money to you or me, but to a family living in poverty it makes all the difference.

Just imagine how many lives could be saved today by promotions on the television or radio. Advertisements by Concern, Trocaire or Goal appeal to our sense of guilt. People will dial a number and offer help. The media is a powerful resource, one which can help us in eliminating hunger. People in the limelight (check out Bill Gates!), have set an example for us to follow. Minutes after the horrifying earthquake struck Haiti, televisions were reporting on the disaster. Everyone around the globe was informed by radio stations, whether they were outside a post office, in school, at home or working. It is unacceptable that a difference in longitude and latitude is the difference between life or death to another person. This is why we must use all our resources to the best of our ability. We must strive to do better next time around in order to achieve our Millennium Goals.

However, not everyone can afford to give money to NGOs, but there are hundreds of other ways to help. For example, swap the Nestlé bar for a Fairtrade bar of chocolate. Reduce your carbon footprint to end droughts. Keep up to date on the latest news, statistics or reports regarding any developments. More than one billion people worldwide are excluded from the minimum acceptable way of life in the state where they live. Times are hard for too many people, too many conflicts continue around the world, too many people are left behind. The world looks to me and you to stop at once and end all this madness. We must unite and prove to generations to come that this is what we did: we eradicated hunger and poverty in 2015. This is what the history books will remember us for, or blame us for if we fail.

I ask you for the final time, before you tuck into your warm dinner and before going to bed tonight think of the forty people who have died by the end of this essay. Together we can and we will eradicate poverty by 2015. In 2015 when you meet here again we will raise a glass and cheer, because we will know mankind is happy at home tonight. We must never give up. Thank you for listening, and please remember that hope and history rhyme.

Passages/Extracts/Quotes
– Senior Category

Gabrielle O'Donoghue

Loreto Secondary School, Fermoy,
Co. Cork, Ireland, Age 17

MDG 2 – Achieve Universal Primary Education

Presidents, Prime Ministers, Kings, Queens and Distinguished Guests, I come before you today with a frank request. I come before you to appeal for your commitment to meeting the Millennium Development Goals. I come before you with the hope that you will approach these ideals with renewed vigour, passion and enthusiasm. Change is in the air ladies and gentlemen. I can feel it, you can feel, each and every one of us here can feel it. Too many years have passed aimlessly by and it is time for progression. The world is calling out for your help. I come before you certain that you will answer their pleas.

Ladies and gentlemen, we are people of all political persuasions but we share a common bond. We are privileged in one respect, united by education. We have spent the best years of our lives in classrooms, striving to fulfil our own individual potential. Simply take a look around this room-would you have achieved such professional success without a solid intellectual foundation? We are the lucky ones. Millions of children worldwide do not have the opportunity to experience this miracle.

Primary education reaches far beyond the tired ideological policies of left and right. Instead, it transcends race, religion, nationality and gender. It is a part of any country's "survival kit". Certainly, in order to survive, people must be educated. Everyone here will agree that personal development and accomplishment form the basis of any civilised society. If this is the case, then our society is about to turn chaotic. If we cannot provide even the most basic primary level education to all members of our global village, then we should be ashamed of ourselves. Is there any trace of humanity within us? It is unacceptable that we are failing miserably in achieving Goal 2: to make sure that all children start and finish primary education. I stumbled across some startling statistics recently and they shocked me to the very core of my being. One in six adults worldwide is illiterate, and around 115 million children around the world receive no schooling at all. Achieving universal primary education enrolment, enrolment not completion, would cost an additional $9 billion every year. Yes, these figures are staggering but wouldn't it be worth it? It is time to take the plunge, the plunge into primary education.

Ladies and gentlemen, please close your eyes. Imagine that you are a ten-year old child living in the developing world. The sun beats down from the azure sky and the heat scorches your back. You are surrounded by desert, consumed by despair. The sand dunes stretch relentlessly beyond the horizon, trapping you. There is no end in sight to this confinement just like there is no end in sight to your suffering. Your world is one of limited opportunity, of hardship and labour. The cattle in the fields are skeletal and the ploughs remain idle. You do not know how to farm the land but you do know that this is where your future lies. Imagine your horror when you discover that you will never go to school, you will never learn to write your name or read your siblings a bedtime story. Now, open your eyes. It is hard to imagine that this terror is in fact reality. It is time to face the music, and it is hardly a symphony.

The famous Irish poet William Butler Yeats once said: "But I, being poor, have only my dreams. I have spread my dreams under your feet; tread softly, because you tread on my dreams." His words epitomise what is happening in the world today. By falling short of the Millennium Development Goals, we are trampling, hindering and demolishing the dreams of the children in the developing world. That is a fact. Based on current rates, 47 million children will still not be in school by 2015. The truth hurts and it pains me to say that these figures demonstrate the world's resolute failure in helping its most needy.

… Finally, I come before you, the leaders of the nations of the world, to appeal for your enthused commitment to reaching Goal 2. Do not waste this opportunity to make a difference in the lives of millions. Together, we could create a legacy that will be passed on from generation to generation, from young to old. That legacy is education. We could be heroes in the eyes of the world, the inspirational people who fought against illiteracy, negativity and poverty. Here today, you could make history by making sure that all children start and finish primary school. The time has come to make a change. It is hanging over us. I can feel it.

Vu Lan Nguyen

St. Joseph's Institution, Singapore, Age 16

MDG 1 – ERADICATE EXTREME POVERTY AND HUNGER

Humbled as I am today by the task before us, I would like to first remind you all of a critical point in humankind's history. Ten years ago, the world stood at a significant crossroad. The third millennium had just arrived, carrying on its wings the novel promises of a new epoch. This was a time ripe for change, and thus the world saw the largest gathering of world leaders in history up until that point – the Millennium Summit. Together, they envisioned a new future, where humanity would be freed from the shackles of extreme poverty, hunger, illiteracy and disease, and thus made eight solemn promises now known as the Millennium Development Goals – in other words, a blueprint for a better world. The first – and also the most fundamental MDG – was the pledge to halve, between 1990 and 2015, the proportion of people living in extreme poverty and suffering from hunger.

Today, we are standing at a similar crossroad. World leaders again gather here to review what we have and have not done, and what we must do with only five years left. A decade has just passed us by, during the course of which we have made important progress in the MDGs in general, and in the first MDG specifically. However, we have been moving too slowly to meet our goals. The challenges that return with a vengeance every generation, such as poor economic growth, social and political unrest, climate change, diminished resources, fewer trade opportunities and reductions in aid flows from donor nations, all contribute to the fact that we are tragically falling behind in our promise.

... Last year, the world found itself in an economic crisis that was unprecedented in its severity and global dimension, which has stalled or even reversed the encouraging trend in our fight against poverty and world hunger. Nothing less than the future of humanity is at stake, and as things are now, if we don't do something soon we may have to watch helplessly as the most foundational MDG continues to slip out of our grasp.

That is exactly the reason why we are here, though – to put our hearts and minds into preventing it from happening. Why am I only referring to the first MDG, you may ask? It is not simply because it plays an essential part in achieving all the other MDGs. To be honest, it actually affects me at a much more personal level. Let me tell you a story.

Twenty years ago, there was a ten-year-old boy living in a rural village in Vietnam. He had seven siblings, and the family was so poor that they had to eat yam with salt just to survive. When his friends were busy dreaming about what they wanted to do, he was busy feeding chickens and ducks. When world leaders con-templated big things like *world* hunger, he contemplated how he would be able to ease *his* hunger, day by day. Then came Viet-nam's investment in agricultural research and extension, as part of some attempt to reduce poverty he didn't know of, and his family started to escape the poverty trap. He could continue going to school. He studied as hard as he could. Things began to change. He soared. He escaped the vicious circle, and into the world be-yond, his wings no longer bound by poverty and hunger.

That boy was I. World leaders, I have learnt the hard way how hunger and poverty can affect people, and how the first MDG can really save millions of lives. We can do it, because this is an era of change; in no other era in the world's history would my story be even possible. Thus, today I stand here, to urge you to remember. Remember why you or your predecessors were here ten years ago, and remember why you are here now…

Jessica Maguire

Loreto Secondary School,
Navan, Co. Meath, Ireland, Age 16

MDG 5 – IMPROVE MATERNAL HEALTH

I don't know any of you. I've never seen you. I've never met you. But I do know about you and one of the promises that you keep breaking. This promise affects me directly but affects the most im-portant person to me even more. I can feel this person worry about this broken promise all the time, even though she doesn't really understand what the breaking of it means for her and me.

I have a lot of time to myself and during this time I've learned some things. You should all know them already but it seems that I understand the fifth promise that you made even better than you do ...

A woman dies every sixty seconds during complicated childbirth. That's 529,000 mothers per year. That's 529,000 children orphaned by lack of maternal care every year. My mother may become yet another number in this awful statistic. Almost half of births in developing countries take place without a skilled birth attendant. That ratio rises to 65 per cent in South Asia. Out of 100 women aged 15-40, 30 do not have antenatal care – 46 in South Asia and 34 in sub-Saharan Africa.

Don't you think it's unfair that while a mother in a developed country has a marginal 1 in 4,000 chance of dying during pregnancy or childbirth, a mother in sub-Saharan Africa has a stark 1 in 6 chance of dying in similar circumstances?

... You can all talk, indeed all of your many speeches are delivered with conviction and passion. But yet there is still a lack of action, of actually doing anything. In September 2001, 147 of you said that you would reduce maternal mortality by three-quarters by 2015. That's only five years away ... tick tock, tick tock. Please don't tell me that this was just another of your empty promises, just words to make you look good.

... I'm scared. I am so, so scared, not only for my mother but for me. I need my mum and she's the only one I've got. But you are taking her from me. You have forgotten what promise number 5 means ... but I haven't and I never will. I am helpless, but you are not. I may die and so may my mother. I thought this would be the perfect occasion to remind you all that you can change that. After all, it's what you promised you would do.

I leave this crucial matter in your very capable hands. This case is as simple as black and white, a case of life and death. I know that you understand this. What I need you to do now is hear me....You are listening but I need you to hear.

Yours Faithfully,

Spokesbaby for the Unborn

Eimear Cleary

Ard Scoil Mhuire, Ballinasloe, Co. Galway, Ireland, Age 16

MDG 4 – REDUCE CHILD MORTALITY

Mr. President, Mr. Secretary-General, Ladies and Gentlemen, my name is Kyesi Sarr and I am from the country of Angola which is located in Sub-Saharan Africa.

I am here today to share my story in the hope that it will inspire the 192 states that signed on to achieve the Millennium Development Goals in 2000 to continue the hard work and determination that is needed from the global community as a whole to have these goals achieved by 2015.

I am sixteen years old and the only remaining child in my family. I had a brother and a sister who both died before reaching their fifth birthday. It may seem ironic but I was born in 1993 and by some miracle of God have survived. My sister was born in 1995 and died aged two as a result of contracting measles because my family had no access to immunisation or the medicine she needed. My brother was born in 2000 but died just a few short weeks later of neonatal tetanus disease. Our village is very remote and quite poor so these stories are nothing new. The nearest medical centre is hours away and like my family most people cannot afford to go there so many births and deaths go unreported.

This is why the fourth goal of reducing child mortality is particularly close to my heart. The life expectancy and child mortality rates in Angola are both among the worst ranked in the world so I consider myself very lucky to not only be here addressing you all today but to be alive at all.

Despite a lot of positive progress, child mortality is not declining fast enough to meet the Goal 4 target of reducing by two-thirds between 1990 and 2015 the under-five mortality rate. Children in the developing world are thirteen times more likely to die within the first five years of life than in a developed country.

... In many countries, malnutrition and lack of access to quality primary health care and basic infrastructure, including clean water and sanitation, is causing ill health and death among children. This is something that needs to be targeted on a larger scale globally as it will play a huge part in reducing child mortality rates.

The journey from my rural village in Angola to the UN headquarters here in New York has truly been a life changing and eye opening one.

I believe the most important thing I brought with me was hope because goals are really just dreams with deadlines aren't they? I have a dream for my family, for my country and indeed for the world that someday we won't need summits like this and that we won't have to try and solve these issues because they won't exist. I hope and pray everyday for better futures for children because my brother and sister's were taken away from them. I think the Millennium Development Goals offer hope to countless people around the world even though they mightn't be aware of it.

I would like to take this opportunity to commend all countries on their efforts to date but urge you not to forget there is still a long way to go. These goals are achievable, but it will take continued resolute, creative and determined action from the global community, but as the great Winston Churchill once said: "Success is not final, failure is not fatal: it is the courage to continue that counts."

Dara Jones

Scoil Mhuire, Strokestown,
Co. Roscommon, Ireland, Age 17

MDG 7 – Ensure Environmental Sustainability

… While I could spend hours upon hours going over how little progress is being made towards achieving many of the goals, the Secretary-General has requested that I speak specifically about the goal that I believe to be in most urgent need of your attention. The goal that I have chosen is goal number seven: to ensure environmental sustainability.

The reason that I believe this goal to be in dire need of your attention is that the situation is gradually worsening in this particular area. This particular goal is made up of four different targets: to integrate the principles of sustainable development into country policies and programmes and to reverse the loss of environmental resources; to reduce biodiversity loss, achieving, by 2010, a significant reduction in the rate of loss; to halve, by 2015, the proportion of people without sustainable access to safe drinking water and basic sanitation; and finally, to have achieved a significant improvement in the lives of at least 100 million slum-dwellers.

The problem with these targets, however, is that they are not being evenly met by everyone. Some countries have achieved many of the goals, while others are not on track to realise any. As I said earlier, I call things as I see them and I am not afraid to name names, so please do not be offended if your country is singled out, because you can be sure that you are not the only one struggling to meet the goals.

Bearing that in mind, take the example of the last target that I called out, to have achieved a significant improvement in the lives of at least 100 million slum-dwellers. China has been making good progress to achieving this goal. However, areas needing the most reduction, such as the Sub-Saharan African regions, have yet to make any drastic changes in improving their quality of life.

With respect to the third target, while some progress is being made towards reducing the amount of people without safe drinking water, 1.1 billion people around the world still have none, and it has been estimated that by 2035, three billion people who already live in water-scarce areas will have no access to safe drinking water. Can anyone here listen to those figures, which are staggering by any standards, and still sit on their hands and do nothing, just because their own country has plenty of safe drinking water? The World Health Organisation has reported that meeting this target could cost as little as $8 billion annually, which is only a fraction of what is being paid by many countries here on arms.

Possibly the most topical, and in my opinion the most important, part of goal seven is to reduce carbon dioxide emissions and the consumption of ozone-depleting substances. This ties in with climate change, which is possibly the biggest long-term threat that we face as a species. Let's face the facts: we are slowly but surely destroying the planet. I don't need to go into the details of global warming and climate change with you; it is such a key issue these days that almost everyone is an expert on the subject. I know that many of you here have your own opinions on global warming, and some of you may subscribe to the theory that it has nothing to do with us, that it is just a natural part of the earth's cycle. Perhaps it is, but there is no doubting the fact that we are speeding up the process considerably.

In just 200 years since we became industrialised, we have changed the face of the earth. NASA studies have shown that global temperatures have risen since 1900; the warmest global average temperatures on record have been in the last fifteen years. These statistics directly coincide with an increase in industry, especially in developed countries. Climate change is also hindering the achievement of other goals: a report from the International Food Policy Research Institute projects that in 2050, there will be an additional 25 million malnourished children, compared to a scenario without climate change.

You must give this goal high priority, and make every effort to achieve it within the next five years. The solutions are not a secret: promote recycling, reduce consumption, invest in the development of green technologies. There are massive untapped renewable energy resources out there; invest in research into green technology and cut down on fossil fuels. It's that simple.

Ladies and gentlemen, thank you for listening to me. I hope that I have managed to spur you on to achieving the Millennium Development Goals. If everyone concentrates on getting their country on track to achieving them, I have no doubt that in five years' time we will be celebrating a historic accomplishment.

Shane McKenna

St. Macartan's College, Co. Monaghan,
Ireland, Age 17

MDG 4 – Reduce Child Mortality

Esteemed World Representatives,

No matter what title you may now possess, no matter what reputation you have attained or no matter what accolades you have achieved, at one point in time you were all teenagers, before that you were children and before that babies. Defenceless, innocent, interdependent, not to mention insatiably cute, for the most that is; you were your mother's pride and joy and the apple of your father's eye as you grew to become the strong individuals that I now see before me. However, for many children, sadly, this is not the case. So many are denied the opportunities that we are blessed with, so many are denied the opportunity to simply live. You, as today's leaders, not only have the responsibility to change this but I believe the means to open the doors of life to these kids and to barricade the door of child mortality.

I don't need to tell you that in today's world, the predominant causes of the child mortality are preventable diseases. In addition, I have no doubt that you are aware of the extent of the current situation. Every year, more than 200 million children under five do not receive basic health care and, as a result, over nine million children die annually from the diseases listed. It horrifies me to think that over the course of one typical day, more than 25,000 children die – that's roughly one life every five seconds that ends unnecessarily. Contrary to popular belief, the biggest killers of children worldwide are newborn complications – pneumonia, diarrhoea, and malaria – and yet global funding does not reflect this proportionality.

From my research, I have discovered that there is a shocking imbalance in healthcare spending between high income countries and those still developing. More money is spent on treating those with rarer illnesses in high income countries than is spent on basic healthcare in the latter. There is a clear need to face up to our responsibilities as the already fortunate; we need to look at world priorities and actually proceed to act accordingly. After years of research it has become blatantly obvious that there are several key child survival plans that are both effective and relatively inexpensive in comparison with other national pursuits that many countries undertake. The spread of malaria in Sub-Saharan Africa causes one in six deaths. Simple mosquito prevention and treatment techniques such as sprays, insecticide-treated nets and anti-malarial drugs have been proven to be cost effective measures to combat this. Despite this, only one in three children is treated with these drugs and what's more frightening is that only 8 per cent of children under the age of five sleep under the protection of these specialised nets.

There is one further point I would like to make. Horrific as these diseases are, and as accountable for high child mortality rates as they are, there is a further evil. A morning in the Chinese province of Hunan brings an unimaginable sight of heartbreaking cruelty and unfathomable horror. There, in the gutter of a busy road, lies the mutilated and lifeless body of a baby girl. Nameless and unwanted, the newborn's life has been taken away, her remains violated by the spray of passing buses and bicycles. Where is the ambulance? Why aren't the passers-by stopping? Where are her parents? The simple truth is that they're not coming. In fact, it's quite likely, if not a certainty, that they are responsible. This young girl has become merely another by-product of China's infamous one-child law. I struggle to understand how such a law can exist when such horrific consequences are apparent? There has to be an alternative. Within an estimated 17 million baby girls "missing" from China's population, the world's mortality rate is obviously underestimated.

According to official figures, 97.5 per cent of all aborted foetuses in China are female. Though this statistic may only seem relevant in regards to gender equality, it also has its bearing on child mortality. It is my strong belief that if the one child law was not in place the actual abortion percentage of China would drop dramatically.

Ladies and gentleman, in order to achieve a decrease in child mortality rates globally it is imperative that we act now. The time for waiting is over. I urge you to do your best as the people with power in our world, as leaders to do whatever it takes to save the lives of those who cannot protect themselves the most. I think it's time that like the modern alternative music god "The Fray", we learned "How to save a life"!

Ashling Flanagan

Scoil Mhuire, Strokestown, Co. Roscommon, Ireland Age 17

MDG 2 – ACHIEVE UNIVERSAL PRIMARY EDUCATION

... I'll start by pointing out the obvious: as you all know, education is extremely important. I don't mean that to be successful everybody needs to go to university and obtain a degree in something or other, of course that helps, but what I'm talking about today is your basic education, reading, writing and basic maths. Think about everything you learned during all of your years of schooling. Now, think about all of the little things you did today. Maybe you ordered something in a restaurant or cafe, maybe you had to read a map or a leaflet or brochure about something. Most of you probably take all of these little things for granted, reading and counting and such, but to so many people living in poverty in the world, even these things are out of their reach.

Addition and subtraction was probably one of the first things you learned in school. I doubt if a day goes by that you don't have to use maths for some reason or another, and yet to many people such skills are totally out of their reach. Yes, for many people basic counting is impossible. Can you imagine not being able to count? Imagine not being able to work out what time it will be in fifteen minutes? And yet, for many people, this is a reality even today.

... In Africa, there are 42 million children that don't have access to school, 60 per cent being girls. Most don't start school until between the ages of seven and ten, and even then it's mostly just boys. This is partly due to the fact that, traditionally, girls are expected to stay at home and keep the house and look after children, but also due to the fact that some girls have to get married at a young age.

Although there are many problems that stand in the way of this goal, there are also many things that can be done to achieve it. Obviously, one of the main things standing in the way of education for everyone is money. There's no easy solution to this, but with the cancellation of debt of eighteen highly indebted poor countries in 2005 we're one step closer to cancelling world debt. Even though it's going to be some time before world debt is completely abolished, there's no better time than now to start increasing investment in the improvement of education systems of developing countries. With better education, it would help decrease the spread of disease, and would help create a more skilled workforce, other companies would be encouraged to invest in Africa, creating more employment, and therefore helping decrease their debt. Another important step that should be taken in helping to improve education services is that governments would have to be encouraged to concentrate more on improving education, and to allocate more funds to education. Many governments would be reluctant to start focusing more on education, but if incentives, such as a slight lessening of their debt if they do certain things to improve education were provided, I'm sure you'll agree that they would be far more ready to make improvements.

Claire Benson

Sacred Heart Secondary School,
Clonakilty, Co. Cork, Ireland, Age 16

MDG 4 – REDUCE CHILD MORTALITY

... We're making huge leaps towards our millennium goals: 30 per cent more children are now living to see their fifth birthdays. However, child mortality is still a major issue and we *have* to reach our millennium goal by 2015.

What's infuriating about our high child mortality rates is that we *know* how to reduce them, but we haven't come as far as we could have in the last 10 years.

Perhaps the most upsetting point I encountered in my research was that a child born in a developing country is over *13 times* more likely to die within the first five years of its life than a child born in the developed world

... Gender inequality also has a huge impact on child mortality. In South and East Asia, and the Pacific, more girls die prior to their fifth birthdays than boys. Sex selective pregnancy termination, neglect and discriminatory access to food and medication mean many baby girls don't stand a chance of survival compared to their male counterparts. Highest reductions in child mortality rates have been observed in 40 per cent of households where mothers have a high level of education and basic healthcare. For many mothers, however, education was never much of an option. This is why it is vital that Goal 4 works closely with Goal 3 in combating gender inequality.

It is our duty as UN member states to pull together and help those in need. We cannot forget the poor or the helpless just as we do not forget the rich and independent. Each of us has the potential to be great. Ladies and gentlemen, no more can be asked of us than to achieve our potential.

So, I put it to you, Presidents, Kings and Queens, Prime Ministers and honoured guests, you who are seen as beacons of hope by so many: Achieve your potential and great things will come of it. In doing so, you *can* stamp out child mortality. You *will* save millions of lives and that is no mean feat.

Roisin Ryan

Loreto Secondary School, Fermoy, Co. Cork, Ireland, Age 17

MDG 3 – PROMOTE GENDER EQUALITY AND EMPOWER WOMEN

... Gender equality underpins progress on all the MDGs. Development makes little sense if half the population is prevented from fully benefiting from and contributing to it. We cannot reach any Millennium Development Goal until we have eliminated discrimination against women and girls. Take Goals 1 and 2, for example. How will the first goal, which calls for a massive reduction in poverty, be realised if women are discriminated in terms of property ownership, access to credit and inheritance? How will the second goal, which demands for universal primary education, be achieved if so many girls never go to school at all or drop out early?

Women have a vital contribution to make – to the economy, to better governance, to peace processes, to their communities and their households. Continuing discrimination reduces their contribution, making us all worse off. The achievement of women's rights will benefit not just women but society as a whole. The world has recognised the importance of gender parity. As far back as 1979, the Convention on the Elimination of All Forms of Discrimination against Women was adopted by the UN General assembly and acceded to by 180 states. We have made the commitment, now it is time to follow through.

The advancement and empowerment of women is the only way to build a sustainable, just and developed society. I stand here before you as a woman, a young woman from the developed world. I've been to primary school, I'm in my final year of secondary school, and I look forward to going to college next year. No threat of a forced marriage looms on the horizon. I am in control of my future. But I am in the minority. Seventy per cent of the world's poor are women. As such, they are much less likely to be educated. Two-thirds of the world's 799 million illiterate adults are women. These uneducated girls are far more likely than boys to become marginalised. In general, these women are married young, often against their will, and forced to bear many children. They are discriminated against in access to health care, are much more likely to contract HIV/AIDS, and most often lack independent financial security.

Speaking of financial security, does it seem fair that women do 66 per cent of the world's work – both paid and unpaid – but earn just 10 per cent of the world's income and have access to a meagre 1 per cent of the world's resources? Of course not. This is not just unfair to women, but bad for economic growth. In some developing countries, it is estimated that growth could be increased by one percentage point if barriers to female entrepreneurs were removed. In other states, women own nearly half of all micro, small, and medium enterprises, but they receive less than 10 per cent of the available credit, slowing economic progress. In too many states, women lack the right to own property, which means they have no collateral for a loan. They have no assets whatsoever; they are at the whim of their male counterparts. A positive policy that has been proven to work in countries as diverse as Vietnam and Egypt provides for property deeds with space for both the husband's and wife's names. Such simple steps, if implemented and enforced correctly, can have resounding effects for the poorest of women.

Many of the obstacles to overcoming inequality towards women are rooted in culture. This is not to say that change will never happen as negative attitudes towards women are intrinsically engrained in the fabric of certain societies. It merely means that political commitment at the highest levels is a necessary requirement if this goal is to be realised. This means your commitment is required, ladies and gentlemen. The majority of the states represented here today have dismantled any gender-biased laws, and even implemented new laws to ensure equality. But laws mean nothing without follow through. Strategies for realising the rights to which women are entitled are well documented, but implementation in too many states has been increasingly slow. Legal and political commitments continue to support only a minority of women. The right to vote, to own property, to run a business and receive credit on equal terms as men, to have access to good health care; these rights are alien to the majority of women.

... Cynics around the world proclaim that we have failed as a global community already, that the MDGs are doomed to be just another set of failed targets. But I disagree. I stand here today, surrounded by 192 heads of state, people with the capacity to speed up the implementation of these strategies. You have the capacity to make the change. You have the opportunity to make this world a more equal and more just place. And if you act now, perhaps one day, there will be as many men as women sitting in this assembly.

Stephanie Reid

Loreto College, Foxrock, Co. Dublin, Ireland, Age 16

MDG 3 – PROMOTE GENDER EQUALITY AND EMPOWER WOMEN

... Ten years ago, you made eight promises to the developing world, one of which was to promote gender equality and empower women. With a goal of the year 2015 for the remaining seven goals, a limit of 2005 was placed on the gender parity target. This was an acknowledgement that education for both boys and girls is the first stepping stone for all the other development goals. However, five years after its target, we are still nowhere near achieving this goal. With every 100 boys not attending school, there are 117 girls in the same situation. Until the number of boys and girls in school are equalised, people in the developing world will never be able to possess the necessary knowledge to tackle disease, hunger, poverty and environmental sustainability. This problem must be solved now, five years overdue.

When one looks at world illiteracy, over 66 per cent of the world's 799 million illiterate people are women. Why should it be like this? For every 100 boys in school, there are only 96 girls. The gap becomes even greater at secondary level. Yet it is more important to educate girls. They become much more vulnerable when uneducated than boys. They are exploited through child labour and sex trafficking. They are twice as likely to develop HIV/AIDS as girls with even a small amount of schooling in their past. Not only this, but women are less likely to have social and political standing. In many developing countries, women's rights are still somewhat denied and due to their expected roles in the family and community they often cannot take advantage of their legal rights, or even be aware of them. In turn, this affects their children. Without education, it has been shown that women are less likely to have their children vaccinated and less likely to know basic mothering skills or their rights as mothers. And so, an uneducated woman turns into a chain of uneducated women and a vicious circle of injustice and inequality arises.

This problem needs to be tackled immediately. It is a disgrace that male children would be sent to school instead of a female. Why should this be? In some situations, girls are taken from school on account of the age of marriage and yes, while cultural customs cannot be changed, the public can be made aware of girl's domestic responsibilities and prevention of early marriage and pregnancy can be undertaken. Studies have shown that to educate girls is the most effective way to increase economic production, lower infant and maternal mortality, educate the future generations, improve nutrition and promote health. Mothers who have had some amount of education are twice as likely to send their own children to school. Quite simply, education of women is the key to the solution of many global and socio-economic problems. What I, and I'm sure thousands of other people all over the world are thinking is, why hasn't anything been done thus far when it was thought to be a feasible target five years ago?

... As part of this goal, it is also important to empower women and teach them that they have the same entitlements as men. Women's entrepreneurship should be financed and supported all over the world, women's rights should be guaranteed through legal and constitutional reforms and women's participation in government should be encouraged and enhanced on all levels.

I hope now you can see that this goal, while it may appear challenging, is entirely feasible. Equal education is the key to solving all the other goals and it is time gender disparity became a thing of the past. I urge you – take action now.

Every girl needs this to become a reality.

Michelle Joyce

Loreto Secondary School, Fermoy,
Co. Cork, Ireland, Age 17

MDG 7 – ENSURE ENVIRONMENTAL SUSTAINABILITY

... This is why Goal 7 is so important. My aim today is to show you how important it is that every nation triples its efforts in ensuring environmental sustainability.

Goal 7 caters for improved sanitation and access to safe drinking water. Nearly one billion people still do not have access to safe drinking water and 2.5 billion people, nearly half the population of the developing world, live without adequate sanitation. By improving sanitation and access to safe drinking water this will reduce the time spent collecting water and fuel wood increasing the time available for education. In addition, the lack of energy, water and sanitation services in rural areas discourages qualified teachers from working in poor villages. If you spent five hours every day getting water and fuel, the chances are that education would not be one of your priorities. It is known that education is a very cost effective method of combating diseases, especially HIV/AIDS. It is reported that educated mothers make more use of health care facilities, including the health services that effectively prevent fatal childhood diseases. Worldwide, the risk of a child dying prematurely is reduced by around 8 per cent for each year that its mother spent in primary school. This is why Goal 7 is imperative to the plan to achieve universal primary education, Goal 2 and consequently Goal 4.

Goal 7 aims to reduce the loss of biodiversity. A huge percentage of fisheries stocks are exploited at or above their maximum capacity and several have already collapsed due to over-fishing.

Each year, roughly 15 million hectares of forest are cleared, generally in developing countries, resulting in increases in vector-borne diseases, declining quantity and quality of water, and local climate changes. Imagine your son, daughter, niece, nephew or any young child you know dying because you didn't have enough fuel to boil the water for them. This happens every single day around the world; just because you don't see it happening does not mean that it never happens. It is easy to see how important Goal 7 is in reducing child mortality.

Goal 7 also seeks to achieve significant improvement in the lives of at least 100 million slum dwellers by 2020. About 900 million people are estimated to live in slum-like conditions characterised by insecure tenure, inadequate housing and a lack of access to water or sanitation. There is progress being made in improving the lives of 100 million slum dwellers but what about the other 800 million people living in slum-like conditions? How can we ever really end poverty if we do not significantly improve the lives of every slum dweller?

... There are only five years left, the question is, how far will you go to protect your home and family? Planet Earth is your home and the human race is your extended family, how far will you go to protect it?

Caoimhe Ní Chorcora

Coláiste Íde, An Daingean Uí Chúis,
Co. Kerry, Ireland, Age 16

MDG 1 – ERADICATE EXTREME POVERTY AND HUNGER

Close your eyes and count to six. A child in the developing world has just died.

Presidents, Kings and Queens, Prime Ministers and distinguished guests, I am here today to remind you that under-five mortality is not declining fast enough to meet the Goal 4 target of reducing by two-thirds the mortality rate for children under five years of age by 2015. As I speak, there are far too many children fighting for their lives. They are fighting off preventable and treatable diseases such as pneumonia, diarrhoea, malaria and measles to name a few.

The pace of progress has been far too slow over the years. So, what went wrong? Probably the biggest reason for continuing world hunger is that our world leaders aren't doing enough to tackle the scandal. Despite your repeated promises there seems to be too much talk and too little action. We need to stop the two-steps-forward, one-step-back tango we have been dancing for years. Start marching ahead. The good news for you is that many people have their boots on and are ready to go.

Ladies and Gentlemen, I would like you all to imagine you are hungry but the shops are closed and your kitchen cupboards are empty. Imagine you are sick or that somebody close to you is sick but your doctor won't see you and the pharmacy is not open. Imagine you are really thirsty but the taps in your house aren't working. You may still be unable to imagine what it means to live in poverty but you're getting there. More than one billion people worldwide are living in extreme poverty. When I say this I don't mean they can't afford the latest Wii console or laptop or the biggest plasma screen television. I mean they can't go a day without being hungry because they can't afford to feed themselves, nor do they have the local supermarket to buy clean water. No, in the developing countries if you do not work, you do not eat and therefore cannot support your family. Everyone has the right to an education as it provides the first step on the ladder out of poverty. But there are still about 72 million children of primary school age in the developing world who are not in school at present. As a result of this history will keep repeating itself unless we stop it and make the change.

... So, I am asking you all again, what is taking so long? There are children out there who need us, and you need to lead the way. All it takes is dedication and belief. All the research is done. We know what we need to do. We have all the facts, so let's turn those facts into acts and reduce child mortality for good because, let's face it, what we're doing now is not enough to put patches on an old suit. If we work together and achieve this goal, it is what the history books will remember our generation for – or blame us for if we fail.

Robert Bolton

Douglas Community School, Cork, Ireland, Age 17

MDG 7 – Ensure Environmental Sustainability

Mr. President, Mr. Secretary-General, ladies and gentlemen, it is such a great honour for me to be here today, to speak to you, at a time where you are at the pinnacle of human achievement. You are at a period in time where you can really achieve so much, and a time where human quality of life improves by the day. I must say, it is a credit to you for me to know that so many people care about me. You see, I am gravely ill, but thankfully you are helping me, because in 2000 the largest meeting of heads of state took place, and you agreed on eight Millennium Development Goals, each of equal but high importance. You set targets for 2015, not only hoping to help your own people, but to help me. Ladies and gentlemen, you realised the power was in your hands to change so many lives. I thank you for caring for me, your planet earth.

However, ladies and gentleman, I would to make the point that my health is in serious decline. Although I feel there have been improvements, I know that you still have some worries about climate change. And you have every right to be worried.

You set me as your goal number seven; you made targets to ensure my sustainability and to improve the lives of your own people who live in city slums. Although I feel positive changes have been made, I still feel like you are at war with me. You have used your technology well to improve your people's lives, but I ask you to make that extra leap over the coming years, to help me. I need you to use what your scientists have developed. I need you to use your technology and to change forever the way in which the people in your world.

My delicate eco-system is being disrupted and I'm afraid I cannot cope any longer. My time is running out, and I'm afraid my time is also your time. You spend trillions each year on buying products. Consumerism is becoming a serious problem and life extension is not helping. More and more of you inhabit me. But space is running out. You are the only species that has been able to develop technologies to live longer, but what you don't realise is that I, and many thousands of species, are suffering from human overpopulation. Do you know what the meaning of life is? If the meaning of life is to live longer, then we are all in deep trouble. You will experience food and water shortages. The future is bleak unless you act now, because at the moment 5,000 people die each day from hunger. This is tragic.

... This speech is about environmental sustainability. It is about me. But it is also about you. All of the Millennium Development Goals need to be tackled, but what I would like to stress is that I bear the burden of affecting your progress.

Your first goal was to eradicate extreme poverty and hunger. Ladies and gentleman, I have been around for 4.5 billion years now, and it literally kills me to feel children dying on my soil. Dying from hunger. The minute they are born, they become hungry, and I cry every day, knowing that I cannot provide water for them. I cannot magically grow crops from my infertile soil, and so I depend on your nations to provide services and food for them. Since I begun this speech 15 children have died from hunger.

... Ladies and gentleman, I have in front of me a glass of water. Water is the blood of life. Without it, you would have only three days to live. Water is my blood. It keeps me cool and provides me with moisture. But some parts of my skin, such as the Sahara desert, continue to dry up. Although water is a part of my body, it cannot reach some parts of me, and it becoming worse with the onslaught of global warming. More frightening is that although you have the transport technology to leave my atmosphere and search for water on other planets, some people need to walk miles to get water. Ladies and gentleman, your countries need to help these people. You spend money on trying to find water on mars when in fact water is here right in front of you. I thought I already have provided you with water? I urge you to provide further funding to protect women who every day spend time collecting water for their families.

Thank you, Planet Earth.

Niamh Brady

Scoil Mhuire, Strokestown,
Co. Roscommon, Ireland, Age 17

MDG 6 – COMBAT HIV/AIDS, MALARIA AND OTHER DISEASES

Mr. President, Mr. Secretary-General, Ladies and Gentlemen,

I sincerely wish that my standing before you today could be described as a pleasure. Unfortunately, the purpose of my being here is to serve as a much needed reminder of the promises you all made, of the goals you stood up and said could and would be achieved by the year 2015. I am talking of course about the Millennium Development Goals.

Now I am not here to lecture you, to sand here and berate you as if you were schoolchildren. My goal today is to simply present you with a few of the reasons why it's highly important that greater steps are taken to achieve the Millennium Development Goals. The main issue I would like to discuss with you today is health.

... HIV/AIDS and malaria aren't the only deadly health issues in developing countries. I'm sure all of you regard the birth of your child as a happy moment, possibly the happiest moment in your lives. But in developing countries childbirth is just another risk to a woman's life. It was agreed that by 2015 the maternal mortality ratio would be reduced by three-quarters and there would be a large increase in the number of births attended by skilled health personnel. But of course when we look at the progress to date we'll see that these aims are nowhere near being met. Access to skilled health personnel is as low as ever and the mortality rate for women in labour remains high. Were these aims designed with the sole purpose of making us sound good? It is all well and good making promises but it is vital we see them through. Are we really too lazy to turn childbirth back into the happiest moment of a woman's life, as opposed to the last moment. One in 22 African women die giving birth which is in stark contrast to the one in 7,300 women in developed countries. Every minute a woman dies in labour, and 99 per cent of these women live in developing countries.

In your defense, I'll admit that I'm being a tad harsh – many countries have been making progress. But unfortunately, this isn't enough to meet the targets. A lot of the problems come down to the fact that this is not purely a health issue – problems regarding water, sanitation, nutrition, education, power, communication, transport and infrastructure also need to be addressed if we are to cut down the maternal mortality ratio. But you can't possibly imagine that developing countries can finance this without our help …

… I would like to conclude this speech by asking you all to please take some time to think about what I've said here today. It's crucial that you all leave with a better understanding of how vital it is to achieve the Millennium Development Goals and I urge you to take the necessary steps to achieve them as soon as possible. One in 10 children in developing countries dies before it reaches the age of five; we can do something to stop this.

Mairead O'Sullivan

Loreto Secondary School, Fermoy,
Co. Cork, Ireland, Age 16

MDG 2 – ACHIEVE UNIVERSAL PRIMARY EDUCATION

... Before I begin I would like to ask a question. What is it that everyone here today has in common that has helped us become who we are today? The answer is simple. We have all had the privilege of having a good education.

Not only did you have a primary education but you also had a secondary and third level education as well. Your education has affected your whole life. Without it do you think you would be sitting here today as world leaders? I think not. Do you think it would be possible for someone who has gone through his or her whole life without any form of schooling to secure a well-paid job, someone who is unable to sign his or her name, someone unable to read or even tell the time? Do you think this person will stand a chance in getting his or her voice heard over those who had the opportunity to go to school? Or to put it quite bluntly, will this person stand a chance in becoming a world leader like you here today? If you think this is possible, I give you permission to leave the room now. If you agree with me, I invite you to listen on.

Ladies and gentlemen, I now ask you to think back on your own school days. Did you ever moan about the early mornings? Or complain about the stack of homework you had to do? Did you ever groan about a teacher who needed a personality transplant? If the answer is yes you are not alone (those of you who say no are lying) but did you ever take into consideration how selfish you were? Let me tell you a story of a woman named Triphonie. This woman never had the chance to go to school. As a result she is now unable to secure a worthwhile job. She has two children and because she earns very little money from her job, Triphonie and her family are struggling to survive. As a result she is unable to send her two little girls to school and instead they must work to earn food. She wants her daughters to have a better childhood than the childhood she had, but with their financial difficulties school is not an option.

Triphonie's daughters are just two out of the 73 million children who still have no access to primary education. Do you think it is fair that these children like Triphonie's daughters will never have the chance to learn their times two tables? Do you think it is all right that they will never learn how to write their name, or even have the chance to play hide and seek in the schoolyard with their friends?

… The cost of providing universal primary education is approximately $10 billion a year yet the world spends $1,500 billion on military expenses alone yearly. You just need to lead in the right direction, but I must urge you to *hurry up*. You have given your word that universal primary education will be achieved by 2015. That is exactly four years, eight months and 12 days left yet from what I can see there has been very little progress. These people are relying on you to give them an education. Do you want it on your conscience that the 73 million people this year along with the millions to follow will have no form of education because you were unable to keep your word?

… Ministers, Presidents, Kings and Queens, world leaders, I would like to thank you sincerely for listening to me here today. I would like to think this speech would encourage you to bring about a change. This speech is a plea for your help. You need to turn your promising speeches into enduring action.

Just remember education is a debt the present owes to the future generation. Let us all clear our loans before it is too late.

Grace Kevaney

Loreto Secondary School, Fermoy, Co. Cork, Age 17

MDG 3 – PROMOTE GENDER EQUALITY AND EMPOWER WOMEN

... Every one of the Millennium Development Goals is related to women's rights. Societies and communities where women are not afforded equal rights to men are very likely to fail in their endeavour to achieve the MDG targets by 2015. Millennium Development Goal No. 3 promotes gender equality and empowers women, a goal that each of you promised to promote at the UN Summit 10 years ago. The United Nations Development Programme aimed to eliminate gender disparity in primary and secondary education, preferably by 2005, and in all levels no later than 2015, but 113 of you failed to meet the 2005 target date. I do not wish to ponder on the failed 2005 deadline because I believe that this goal is achievable by 2015 if, today, each and every one of you renew your promises to the women and girls that go mistreated and unrepresented in our countries around the world; if, today, you pledge, once again, to give them a voice and a place in your societies to realize their full potential, in order to be able to contribute meaningfully to each of their societies. I tell you this again: Global peace and prosperity will only be achieved once all the world's people are empowered to order their own lives and to provide for themselves and for their families.

... Not one of the MDGs can be achieved in isolation from or without progress on each of the others. I think that many people here today are unaware of the absolute vitality and importance of gender equality in achieving the Millennium Development Goals. I believe that women's rights are central to the Millennium Declaration and while this is elaborated in Goal 3, all of the goals relate to women's rights. I don't doubt that once women achieve equal rights with men, development will be transformed. Educated girls have better opportunities to work for higher wages. They are more likely to become involved in community life and in decision-making within their communities. They are more educated about health risks such as HIV/AIDS. They tend to marry later and have fewer, healthier children, which they are more likely to send to school. Gender equality is truly vital in your struggle to eliminate poverty to make the world a better place for everybody to live in by 2015.

... As heads of state, how can each of you achieve this goal, and what is it that needs to be done? Firstly, you need to hire more female teachers to act as role models to encourage girls to attend school. Ensure that girls are provided with transportation to and from school. Provide separate sanitation facilities for girl and boys. I think that the enhancement of non-formal education for girls and woman, such as vocational or skills training and literacy programmes, are also vital in your efforts to achieve MDG 3 and, ultimately, eliminate poverty. I believe that women must be given a voice because only then can they truly contribute to society. Try your best to enhance the participation of women at all levels of government. You must set up efforts to implement decent work principles, such as social protection and freedom from harassment. Rwanda is a country that put these points into practice. Rwanda adopted a constitution in 2003 which guarantees a minimum of 30 per cent of parliamentary seats and other leadership positions to women.

... I do not want you going away today with regret for the failed 2005 target or with fear for the work that lays ahead of each of you, because, despite what statistics say, I believe that MDG 3 is a goal that is achievable by the 2015 deadline. I want you to go away today filled with a new hope and encouragement to face that goal that awaits you so that by achieving this goal we are beginning in our task to achieve the Millennium Declaration: to make the world a better place for everybody to live in by 2015.

Sarah Bradley

Presentation College, Tuam,
Co. Galway, Ireland, Age 16

MDG 4 – REDUCE CHILD MORTALITY

... I am going to speak to you about child mortality.

My name is Bahati. I was born in Sierra Leone in August 1993. That is not my real name. I am called Bahati by my parents because Bahati means luck or good fortune. This name was given to me by them because I am now their only surviving child. My two sisters died before they were five years old. I am therefore one of the lucky ones.

You will appreciate, therefore, that my subject is very personal to me. Statistics are often used to quantify the problem of child mortality. However, we should never forget that behind every statistic there are grieving families and communities.

Sierra Leone has one of the lowest survival rates of children in the world. Of the 200,000 children born in Sierra Leone in the year I was born, 54,000 did not make it to their fifth birthday. Compare this to Ireland. Their populations are similar yet here child mortality rate is four per 1,000 births; in Sierra Leone, it is 270 per 1,000 births. The difference in survival rates is staggering.

In September 2000, 189 nations and 147 heads of state and governments promised to achieve eight goals by 2015. One of these goals included reducing child mortality rates by two-thirds. While some progress has been made, it is now likely that this target will not be met.

In 2006, UNICEF Director Ann Veneman said: "The loss of 9.7 million young lives each year is unacceptable, especially when many of these deaths are preventable." I would suggest that instead of the word "unacceptable" she should have used the word "scandalous".

One wonders why these targets will not be met. The most obvious answer is that resources from the wealthier nations have not been forthcoming or have been diverted elsewhere. The funds have probably been allotted to more worthwhile causes such as, fighting wars in Iraq, Afghanistan and Sudan or elsewhere. Maybe they were used to bail out greedy bankers worldwide. This is unfortunate as the causes of the high mortality rates among children are already well documented and are not in need of further research.

... It is a matter of urgency that we at least give a wholehearted attempt to reach this millennium goal. At the moment, the wheels appear to have stopped turning. These people cannot pull themselves out of this hole alone. They need our help, at least to get out.

I am an exception in my country. Firstly, I survived, but secondly, I got out. Whenever I could, I ran. I ran and ran and ran. Then one day, I was noticed. That was the beginning of a whole new life. I was one of the few athletes to compete at championship level for my country. One of my dreams is to make it to the Olympics and win a gold medal in the marathon.

But my main dream is to stop children dying. So I appeal to you. You have the power to at least set the wheels in motion again. There has been a decrease already, but it is not enough. There are five years left, so let's achieve this goal, together. Thank you.

Colm Lawless

Templeogue College, Dublin, Ireland, Age 17

MDG 1 – Eradicate Extreme Poverty and Hunger

I thank you for the generous applause. It is truly an honour to stand here before a sitting of the General Assembly. Many inspirational leaders have delivered powerful orations from this podium. I am deeply humbled to follow in their footsteps. I have arrived in New York to address this audience on the implementation of Millennium Development Goal 1 – the eradication of extreme poverty and hunger.

We inhabit a world today that is conditioned by consumerism and greed. The global banking crisis has precipitated the demise of enterprises across the globe. As we bask in the sunlight pervading through this chamber, we are still reminded of the silhouette of global poverty – pertaining primarily to our own neglect and indifference. Ladies and gentlemen, in the twenty-first century, one in five people live in absolute penury. The situation that exists is a damning indictment of our failure to mobilise on an issue of life or death. President John F Kennedy once declared: "The world is very different now. For man holds in his mortal hands the power to abolish all forms of human poverty, and all forms of human life." Previous generations were incapable of tackling the poverty crisis due to a lack of funds and monetary power. Today we can alleviate a crisis that has plagued the world's population for too long.

... Our irresponsible funding in the field of warfare has been a symbol of our failure. I challenge you, ladies and gentlemen, to provide me with a plausible explanation for expenditure on weaponry, when our brothers and sisters starve to death in some of the most inhospitable parts of this planet? We must divert funding away from military expenditure and progress towards an equitable society. Mutual disarmament must form the underpinning of our objective as a people. Comfort expenses can only be considered when starvation is a feature of the past. At national level, we spend a horrific sum of national income on matters such as tax breaks for the wealthy. Leaders, I cannot over-emphasise my shame on witnessing a crumbling of support for the most vulnerable. As Tony Benn once remarked: "If we can find the money to kill people, we can find the money to help people."

We have faced a plethora of obstacles in our path to world prosperity, ladies and gentlemen. This assembly has mandated us to campaign and achieve our goal. In many nations that are represented here today, wealth is concentrated in the hands of the very few. The UN has demonstrated this as a key consideration in our inability to tackle poverty. It is time for us to reassess and reform our economic priorities. The death of a laissez-faire approach has become apparent and we are now in a position to radically overhaul a flawed system of inequality. In each of our states, we witness the onset of poverty. Our approach appears hypocritical unless we can demonstrate our ability to alleviate the ravages of this phenomenon in a very real manner. Imagine a world that places an emphasis on the disadvantaged. Take this dream and form the realistic basis for a solution.

We may only achieve such a solution on the back of our recent success. I am not here to excoriate any nation's progress. I would be incorrect to assert such a notion. To date, we have achieved a monumental feat – absolute poverty and starvation have been halved in Northern Africa, along with Southern, Eastern and South Eastern Asia. Such achievements are testament to the diligence of every single representative at this General Assembly meeting this morning. Much has yet to be accomplished, however. We must concentrate on the troubled regions that have not been addressed. These include Oceania, Sub-Saharan Africa, Latin America, Western Asia and the former Soviet bloc. I can assert that the leaders of these states have been working to achieve the Millennium Goal that we have all agreed to implement. The primary stagnation in achieving the Goal in these countries lies in the fact that we have not sufficiently co-operated. The European Union, along with the United States, has a major role to play in cementing progress in such regions.

Leaders, when we return to our respective countries, we tend to focus on national issues as the primary consideration in our duty as officials. In order to integrate as a people and co-operate to the extent of eliminating the major obstacles that halt our development, we must begin to look outwardly. Only when we understand that world issues have a direct impact on our domestic lives may we truly embrace the essence of our task at hand …

Robert Boland

St. Gerard's College, Bray, Co. Wicklow,
Ireland, Age 17

MDG 2 – ACHIEVE UNIVERSAL PRIMARY EDUCATION

Mr. President, Mr. Secretary-General, Ladies and Gentlemen, to-day I am here to talk to you about the dream that's hidden deep inside of me, you and everyone else around us.

You and I have this burning desire in our hearts to achieve a certain goal before our time on this earth has passed. It may be a childhood dream to become an astronaut, or to experience the sheer thrill of terror and rush of adrenaline as we dive out of a plane at 20,000 feet. Inside each of us there is a dream, a goal in our lives that's hidden deep down in the very crevices of our souls just waiting to get its chance in the world. Martin Luther King had a dream and he let the whole world know about it; never before had we experienced such a passionate outburst of emotion that grabbed the world's attention and really shook us to the core.

Ten years ago, I listened to you all as you poured out your emotions, opinions and your dreams. I had every faith in you, the most powerful people on the planet, that you would achieve these goals no matter what. You would not be alone as I and everyone else on this planet would be there with you, to help you leap over every hurdle, destroy any barriers and dodge all obstacles in your paths, just to achieve our eight goals, our dreams.

"Let us think of education as the means of developing our greatest abilities, because in each of us there is a private hope and dream which, fulfilled, can be translated into benefit for everyone and greater strength for our nation." These were the words of President John F. Kennedy, a man of action, a man of courage and a man with goals. What's more, he achieved his goals. There is no reason why the assembled 189 heads of state here today cannot achieve eight simple goals. I know you all have your own individual, talents, strengths, resources and abilities. Some of us may not be as lucky as others; as individuals we may be weak, but as one we are unstoppable. We all bring something to the table and we must all play our part if we want to achieve our goals. Each one of us is part of the solution; we are all like the pieces of a jig saw puzzle. We cannot complete the puzzle without every single last piece.

The world is grossly imbalanced. To achieve universal primary education worldwide; it would cost $10 billion dollars. You may think that sounds like a lot, but it's not. Americans spend more than twice that on ice cream every year. Now I'll let you decide for yourselves which is more important, the education of today's youth or to satisfy the cravings of Americans plagued with obesity?

There is more to this matter than sending children to primary school. "The direction in which education starts a man will determine his future life." Education is essential to our future in life, our career choices, decisions that we make and securing the futures of others. Education sets us on a path for life. Who knows how my life would have turned out if I had not been fortunate enough to receive education from such a young age?

"Education is not preparation for life, education is life itself." From the very moment we first come into this world, our brains are taking in everything around us, studying, analysing and filing away information. If little else, the brain is simply an educational toy. A constant hunger lingers in our souls, not for food, however, but for knowledge and information. We have to do our best to satisfy our relentless thirst for knowledge and the best way to do this is to achieve universal education.

Education not only feeds our minds but also has an unlimited number of benefits, not only for ourselves but also for the others around us. Today's youth are less likely to be involved in crime and antisocial behaviour if their minds are kept occupied. Young people who have completed primary education are over 50 per cent less likely to contract HIV than those who have missed out on an education. Universal education could prevent up to 700,000 new cases of HIV each year since about 30 per cent of all infections are in this age group.

Education is the first step in solving several of the world's major problems; it's almost like killing two birds with the one stone …

Shikha Shahi

Uttar Pradesh, India, Age 18

MDG 1 – ERADICATE EXTREME POVERTY AND HUNGER

Mr. President, Mr. Secretary-General, Ladies and Gentlemen,

Good Morning. It is my great honour to address you today on the 65th session of United Nations General Assembly. Please allow me express my admiration and respect for the positive work you all have done and initiatives you all have taken to make this world a better place.

You all serve as an inspiration to many across the world and a lot of people aspire to be like you and make a difference.

My name is Mohandas Karamchand Gandhi and I come from India. Please don't be alarmed by my presence here. I am not a ghost and I am not an apparition. I am merely a memory – a memory residing in the minds of the people who have kept me alive in their hearts for so many years after my death. For this I am grateful.

I have been invoked here today to address you all on an issue which has plagued us all for a long time – poverty.

I wish I could call poverty a disease. Then we could work out a cure and eradicate it from the face of earth. But it is not a disease. It is a state of being so that every hope, every dream, every initiative is wiped out. It is a state where a person is so poor that he sees his loved one die – of hunger, of illness, of abuse – right in front of his eyes and knows that he can't do anything to stop it. Can you imagine such a thing happening to you? Of being so helpless that you see your mother, your child, your wife, your friends die but know that all you can do is wait and watch because there is no one out there who cares, no one out there who is willing to help.

I, in my youth, have seen too much misery and too many people die of starvation. I took the vow of poverty, and since that time consecrated my life to helping the poor and the downtrodden. The job satisfaction was seeing the smile on people's face, my salary seeing hope reignite in people's eyes, and their belief in God returning.

Today, all the initiatives you have taken are doing the same thing for people, bringing joy back in their lives. What makes it great is the fact that it is not done for personal benefit but for the love of mankind and a genuine desire to help humans out of their misery.

Your Millennium Development Goals are proving to be extremely useful in focusing attention on and thereby mobilising resources to deal with the problem of global poverty. They have also resulted in the formulation of many policies, both at the global and at the national level, to reduce the poverty prevailing in various countries. This combined with the pressure on leaders to meet the targets as set by United Nations in order to be at par with the development taking place in rest of the world has resulted in lot of positive steps being taken in order to eradicate poverty.

But even with all the great work being done, and all the positive steps being taken, I believe there is a need to re-evaluate and check if there is something more that can be done, another step that can be taken, perhaps? ...

174

SOUNDBITES – SENIOR

Carol Shanley

Rice College, Ennis, Co. Clare, Ireland, Age 16

MDG 8 – DEVELOP A GLOBAL PARTNERSHIP FOR DEVELOPMENT

... The Millennium Development Goals were agreed and signed off in 2000. Since then, while there have been significant advances in debt relief, combating the HIV/AIDS virus and other diseases, and in other areas, there is still a considerable amount of work to do. It is important to realise that we as individuals can assist the achievement of these goals, not just by lobbying Government to bring about change. We can also help non-government organisations working in these areas to achieve their targets too. For example, assisting Concern with their work by fundraising is assisting in the attainment of the Millennium Development Goals.

The deadline for the Millennium Development Goals may be five years away, but it is only five years away.

Alyssa Liljequist

Homeschool, Newberg, Oregon, USA, Age 16

MDG 1 – ERADICATE EXTREME POVERTY AND HUNGER

... For many in affluent countries, it is difficult to even grasp what many people in other parts of the world are forced to live with on a daily basis. While we eat pounds of meat, there are children who only weigh a few pounds; 30,000 people die of starvation *every day*. This is a great tragedy. There are those who are overwhelmed by the statistics and choose to try to ignore the problem. But we cannot – and we must not – choose ignorance or apathy. No matter how well some of us are acquainted with the enormous problem of world hunger, we can all use a reminder. These are not simply statistics. These are not just numbers on a page. These are precious human beings. They all have a story.

Niamh Heavey

Scoil Mhuire, Strokestown,
Co. Roscommon, Ireland, Age 17

MDG 7 – ENSURE ENVIRONMENTAL SUSTAINABILITY

... Are your comforts so important to you that you will risk the welfare of your own future generations and the future of your planet? Is there a point in preaching without practicing? If your answer to these questions is yes, then I will be forced to question your role in the world as a leader. The welfare of the environment should be the number one priority of all human's list. Our own welfare is in question were anything to happen to it. Not every end is a goal, but to put an end to even *some* of the environmental issues facing us today would be a major step towards the preservation of life on earth. In light of the facts that we have been faced with nowadays, there are a lot of solutions we have, which are not always practiced, but there are also a lot of solutions yet to be discovered. If we use what we already know and make at least one small change in our everyday lives to improve our environment, we could, in the future, be saving somebody's life and the planet's survival.

176

Jin Rui Yap

Tunku Abdul Rahman College,
Selangor, Malaysia, Age 18

MDG 1 – ERADICATE EXTREME POVERTY AND HUNGER

We sit together here today, comfortable in our cushioned seats, in this air conditioned room. In this day and age, mankind has crossed many borders, and gone so far. With all our advancements noted and commended, you would think that no one would have to look at poverty in the eyes. Yet in another part of the world, right now, a man is out on the streets, begging for food that he will use to feed his family later. A woman stands in a dark alley, clutching a coat hanger that drips with the blood of her unborn child. At this very moment, an under aged child is labouring to generate income in order to subsist.

Ladies and gentlemen, we have blood on our hands.

Daniel McFadden

Pobalscoil Chloich Cheannfhaola,
Falcarragh, Co. Donegal, Ireland, Age 17

MDG 1 – ERADICATE EXTREME POVERTY AND HUNGER

… Sometimes it falls upon a generation to be great, a generation that really makes a difference. We can be that generation. Of course this task will not be easy. But not to do this would be a crime against humanity, against which I ask all humanity now to rise up. Those of you who feel they need to be inspired, think of the face of a malnourished child in Ethiopia handed life-saving food supplies. Think of the face on a mother as much needed medical supplies arrive which will mean her child's survival. Think of the face on a child as they are handed their first book and suddenly realise their future will be much brighter. Let this moment be the daybreak in your mind. Let this moment be the sunrise to end a long dark night that was your way of thinking. No longer will you think this is the way it has to be, people will no longer have to suffer extreme poverty and hunger. From this day forward our main goals must be to first of all believe we can change and then make other people believe that we are capable of making this change. Then together we can free the world from poverty and hunger.

Helen Dinan

Loreto College, Fermoy, Co. Cork, Ireland, Age 17

MDG 5 – IMPROVE MATERNAL HEALTH

… I realise that some of you may think that I am only a 17-year-old girl who's biggest problems are boys, spots, clothes and make-up, and you would be partially right. However, some day I wish to have my own children and would be greatly distressed if I didn't have access to the services and facilities I needed, and so I feel that if I would need them, doesn't every pregnant woman and girl in the world deserve the proper facilities and services to have a healthy and happy pregnancy? No matter where they're from or their background, motherhood should be a positive and fulfilling experience and not associated with the fear of death. So yes, I am a 17-year-old girl who has the worries of most other 17-year-old girls, but I am using my voice to give a voice to those who have none. I am only one person what can I do? But together we can do anything.

Aisling McGing

Davitt College, Castlebar, Co. Mayo, Ireland, Age 18

MDG 1 – ERADICATE EXTREME POVERTY AND HUNGER

According to the Universal Declaration of Human Rights: "All human beings are born free and equal in dignity and rights. They are endowed with reason and conscience and should act towards one another in a spirit of brotherhood." This does not seem to have happened. If we acted towards one another in a spirit of brotherhood then there would be no poverty. There would be no need. We would share our wealth and the world would be a better place. I know that sadly it is an unreasonable expectation but I dare to dream of a world were this is true.

There is a song by John Lennon called "Imagine". Some of its lyrics go: "Imagine not positions, I wonder if you can, no need for greed or hunger, a brotherhood of man." This is what I imagine the future will be for my children.

Jessica Earl

Bandon Grammar School, Co. Cork, Ireland, Age 18

MDG 4 – REDUCE CHILD MORTALITY

... This goal should be re-named "raising child survival" rather than "reducing child mortality", as mortality rates can never be lowered enough. Death is an unequivocal part of life and the human condition and preventing the deaths of every child is nearly impossible. Raising survival rates for children, however, is far more tangible and achievable. By improving the chances for survival for children under five you are opening up possibilities and creating a future for these children who may one day sit where you sitting now and represent you or make similar decisions about your fate!

There are those who may be disillusioned by the enormity of the goals, but remember – most of this work involves only simple preventatives and co-operation. And if a good start is half the work, then be glad that a good start has been made! As long as the process has been started you can now up the ante and achieve the aim that you all agreed to ten years ago.

Cara Halliday

Wallace Hall Academy, Dumfries,
United Kingdom, Age 16

MDG 2 – ACHIEVE UNIVERSAL PRIMARY EDUCATION

I look back on my time in primary school with fond memories. Taking my new lunch box into school to show off to my friends, the sense of achievement when you do well in the maths test you have been worrying about for days and the feeling after you win the sack race at sports day. I remember my primary years as being both exciting and scary, but that's the way it's meant to be. Teachers will nag, friends will come and go, homework will be forgotten, and forms to be filled in will return a week late. Primary school is for discovering yourself. The child will grow and develop into someone very unique and confident. Without primary school, the child is denied their childhood and that is where it all goes on. Where does a child end up if they don't start at the beginning? Nowhere.

It is a real shame that millions of unfortunate children over the world are being denied this wonderful time in their lives. We need to make sure something is done to change it.

Stephanie Okolo

Loreto College, Swords, Co. Dublin, Age 16

MDG 6 – COMBAT HIV/AIDS, MALARIA AND OTHER DISEASES

World leaders, I know this is a very challenging project to complete, but do not forget your promises. For as they say, "it's better not to promise than promise and fail", so don't regret doing this, leaders of today, as you are creating a foot path for tomorrow's leaders to walk …

I know we are trying a lot, but we need to go further; this isn't how we started, is it? In 2000 we were more motivated in promoting this project than we are now and *no,* we shouldn't blame events such as the recession for our lack of concern, because the recession is nothing compared to the millions of deaths caused by these curable diseases!

Part Three

ADULT CATEGORY

(over 19 years old)

Extract from speech given by
An Taoiseach Bertie Ahern

United Nations Millennium Summit, September, 2000

...The statistics of poverty and inequality in our world are shocking and shameful: half the world's population struggling on less than two dollars a day; over a billion on less than one dollar; a quarter of a billion children of 14 and under working, sometimes in terrible conditions; and death from preventable and treatable diseases – 10 people will die of malaria in the five minutes I take to address the Assembly.

There was much talk some years ago of a new world order. A new order is indeed dawning. The capacity of globalization to transform our economies and societies is enormous. But, unless shaped by a value system, globalization will mean an ever more lopsided world. The level playing field will remain an illusion so long as a majority of players are ill-fed, ill-trained and ill-equipped.

Perhaps the phrase "fair world order" sums up better what we should strive for. It recognizes that we live in a society, not a market place. It admits of concepts of justice and human solidarity. It acknowledges that, while not everyone will live in the same way, we are all entitled to dignity and decency.

First Place – Adult

Gerard Foley
Dublin, Ireland

**MDG 6 – Combat HIV/AIDS,
Malaria and Other Diseases**

Mr. President, Mr. Secretary-General, Ladies and Gentlemen, I thank you for this opportunity this evening, to come before you to speak on such an important topic. Ten years ago, at the turn of the millennium, we came together in unprecedented unity to address some of our world's greatest problems, health, poverty, education, equality, environment. On that special occasion, we established the Millennium Development Goals. These goals were not careless lip-service, they were a solemn promise. They were, and still remain, real objectives, with real measurements and outcomes, and perhaps most importantly, they came with a real deadline. We are only five years from that deadline. While our MDGs cannot in reality be separated from one another, I am here tonight to specifically address goal number 6, which was our promise to overcome the burden of disease, a burden which afflicts so many people, and yet so unnecessarily. In this self-imposed race against disease and inequality, we have started well, but we have also floundered. As we approach this final leg, now is the time to show our resolve as a united people.

Health is one of the fundamental cornerstones of human rights, and so by definition it is a universal right for all, without respect to age, geography, creed or colour. It is therefore our responsibility to guide the protection and promotion of health for everyone. And yet we are failing. Even now as I speak, a child is dying every 30 seconds from Malaria, every 14 seconds another child is orphaned and deprived of their family through HIV/AIDS, and still every 15 seconds that passes another person succumbs to the ravages of tuberculosis. Besides the horrifying reality revealed by every passing minute, these people share another common thread, these human tragedies are all preventable.

We live in a time when medicine and its application have reached an unprecedented pinnacle. New drug discovery is at an all time high, and for the most part, so is investment and funding. Biomedical research has become expansive, and the potential it contains is, again, at an exceptional level. While this bodes extremely well for the future of biomedicine in itself, the question has now shifted from "Can we prevent...?" to "Why are we *not* preventing...?"

And certainly, the feedback from MDG 6 to date makes for concerned reading. I will not overly expound upon numbers, especially numbers that many people here this evening will understand and appreciate far better than I. However I would like to draw attention to at least some of these disquieting results.

Of the two million deaths that were attributable to HIV/AIDS worldwide in 2008, Sub-Saharan Africa accounted for 1.2 million, or 70 per cent of those deaths. Considering this region comprises only 10 per cent of the world population yet accounts for 67 per cent of those people living with HIV/AIDS, it is simply unacceptable. And yet Sub-Saharan Africa can only lay claim to a mere 3 per cent of global health workers, while in stark contrast, North America has over 42 per cent of health workers.

In Eastern Europe and Russia, the newly diagnosed cases of HIV have grown almost exponentially since the year 2000, the same year we implemented the MDGs. More worrying is that this bloom of HIV is showing no signs of slowing down.

However the MDGs are not simply a target for naysayers and failure, for they have also brought success, and if it is in those bad stories that we steel our preserve, it is in these good stories that we must garner optimism and persevere onward towards our ideals. And without doubt, the MDGs have provided good stories.

In Latin America and the Caribbean, there has been an almost 40 per cent reduction in the incidence of tuberculosis over the last 10 years, and in even Sub Saharan Africa there has been a small but significant drop in HIV/AIDS prevalence. There are also positive indications on the strengthening of health systems and their ability to detect, diagnose and record disease.

Statistics can and will be argued over indefinitely, but we must see past the numbers and graphs and tables to realise that they represent real people. People versus numbers, a cliché we have all heard time and again, but I plead that you do not idly disregard it. As unpleasant and sometimes difficult as it can be to put a face with some statistic, it is also the greatest impetus we have at our disposal. Even with my relative inexperience working with these issues, I have seen the atrocity of inequality. I have seen people die before me because they don't have access to the most basic of medicines, I have borne witness to those literally wasting away only for the lack of a certain pill or tablet, and I have observed people who have contracted the most serious of diseases only for the want of simple knowledge and education. They are unforgiving and inescapable images, but they are also inspiration, inspiration to overcome and conquer the health problems our world endures.

As with any undertaking of this magnitude, the Millennium Development Goals have had their pitfalls and disappointments just as much as they have shown us success and reason for hope. And we will continue to both win and lose these skirmishes with disease and health, but we must never lose sight of the overall victory that is within our grasp. If we are to stay the course and realise the convictions we made to ourselves and others a decade ago, we must be adaptable. There have been innumerable suggestions and critiques of Millennium Goal 6, but I would like to mention, if I may, some of those that I personally find compelling

There is an ongoing need to increase funding and revise policy. Throughout the time of the MDGs, expenditure and funding has increased, there is no doubt about that. While this is an achievement in itself, the fact, however, remains that health expenditure in low-income countries remains insufficient to realise the goals by 2015. That said, simply making more money available will not suffice. We need more funding, yes, but more than that, we need *smart* funding. Improvements and alterations of policy at every level are required, and trade negotiations and embargoes need to be revisited and revised. With the added expenditure and complexity these revisions entail, improved leadership and governance must go hand in hand.

Improvements and strengthening of health systems are a necessity. Although progress is being made with the health systems of countries, many still fall *far* below adequate. If more money was added to some of these already-fragile systems, they would simply not benefit due to inefficiency, poor co-ordination or broken communication with partners. Again, revision is necessary if we are to solidify and create robust, durable systems. Strong health systems are not only vital for the future, but also for current monitoring. We cannot properly track our progress if we have unreliable or even missing data. We also need these country systems to improve upon accessibility, to reach out beyond the major cities. Some of our intervention programmes need to be vastly improved, and again, access is of the highest importance. Even if we have the best people on the ground, the latest equipment and the best methods, I ask you, what good is an intervention programme if it is not reaching the people in need?

On the last suggestion I will raise, there is a drastic need to both increase the number and balance the distribution of health workers. The ratio of health staff in some of the areas most affected by disease is appallingly skewed. To such an extent in fact, it has become one of the greatest limitations in scaling up human health to achieve MDG 6. It has been estimated that worldwide, we need approximately 4.5 million *more* trained people to meet the challenges of health promotion and protection. Multiple reasons have been proffered for this deficiency; that professionals are unhappy with the poor conditions of their jobs, that they are seeking better pay in private sectors, and that they are migrating to other countries. While this grave issue has attracted much attention, and while some solutions have been put forward, the overall problem has yet to be approached in the holistic and significant manner that it demands.

In closing, I will say that there are no magical answers, nor solutions that can be made to fit all. Our challenges are numerous, and can only be matched by their complexity. Ten years ago we overcame the biggest hurdle – we set out our definite aims and objectives with the MDGs and in so doing took our first step. We started a fire that burns bright with hope. It is now up to us, as it has always been, to either fan those flames with our sincerest efforts, or allow our ideals to wane and fade with that fire.

Ladies and gentlemen of the assembly, I hope my voice has found resonance here this evening. I thank you for your attention.

SECOND PLACE – ADULT

Flynn Coleman
New York, United States

MDG 3 – PROMOTE GENDER EQUALITY AND EMPOWER WOMEN

Mr. President, Mr. Secretary-General, Ladies and Gentlemen,

Imagine for a moment that I could tell you about one, just one, of the Millennium Goals, and that if this goal were achieved then the rest of them would be realised as well.

This hallowed hall, where you, the 192 Heads of State, come together to decide the fate of your populations, is the only organ where all UN members have equal representation. Further, a majority of you represent most of the nations on this planet, namely, the developing ones. Now picture the whole world patterned this way.

On March 8th, the world marked the 100th International Women's Day. Women now earn half of the science degrees conferred, yet their share of academic leadership positions, Nobel prizes and high paying jobs in fields like computer science and engineering reveal a large discrepancy between their abilities and their ultimate rewards as compared to their male counterparts.

Women are the gatekeepers of their villages' environmentally sustainable techniques and the secrets of motherhood. They have a deep knowledge of their eco-systems and are the primary water gatherers, cooks, domestic organisers and healing agents for their families.

Yet these same individuals, who work the land and understand its bounty, rarely have access to it as landowners in the developing world, most often retaining no property rights whatsoever, even though their labour is what sustains its vitality. Colonisation may be fading, but its cultural, societal and legal effects still yield incredible force; and those who lost the most in that game were women, who sometimes held power in pre-colonial eras, like the elderly *Bantu Tirki* women of Western Kenya, who could ask for permission to express their opinions in dispute settlements.

When a mother receives a malaria net or a course on sexual education, she shares the net with her babies and an understanding of HIV/AIDS transmission with her partner and her friends. When we equip the millions of single mothers with opportunities to nurture their families while joining the workforce, they will raise a healthy generation of powerful women and respectful men who understand the world around them.

When the baby does arrive on this earth, she is enormously more likely to be healthy and to flourish when her mother has received proper pre-natal care, often given by midwives and other women with a vast reservoir of expertise regarding infants. If she has an income, self-esteem and a voice in community decisions, she is more likely to be able to support her children and use contraception.

In fact, the UN already knows about utilizing the unique skill sets of women to instil peace and positive change; Nigeria and India have both sent record numbers of women to Liberia to serve as catalysts for diplomatic change in peacekeeping missions. Incidents of rape have decreased, and while the system is still evolving, the female presence is softening mentalities and lifting up a place ravaged by war, famine, violence and hate.

India has continued to pioneer the trend by taking the visionary step of allotting one-third of the legislative seats to women. The country will become a model for what can be achieved when women are intricately involved in the democratic process.

In Chile, women formed a collective in the wake of the era of disappearances in order to heal from their grief and to take part in business skills workshops. All the while they created *arpilleras*, small cloth swatches sewn with beautiful bold colours and designs, each telling a story of a mother's loss, a wife's pain, a sister's agony or a daughter's longing. These workshops allowed the women to find comfort in each other and to gain fulfilling jobs, while detailing the stories of their kidnapped loved ones so that the truth would prevent future atrocity.

Armed with a voice in community discussions, political decisions and leadership roles, women will rise above their poverty and their pain. Most importantly, they will bring their children, husbands, brothers, mothers and friends with them. Women will invest the skills they learn in business school back into their towns and teach sustainable living to their children, ensuring environmental protection for the next generation.

In 1976, Wangari Maathai started planting trees to reverse deforestation and poverty. This community initiative, the Green Belt Movement, began to dramatically enhance the lives of the women involved. Maathai became the first East African woman to earn a doctorate and the first African woman to win the Nobel Peace Prize. The programme created skills training along with lush vegetation and natural havens that decrease the hours that women need to spend collecting food and firewood, freeing time for learning, starting careers and even time to explore passions, not to mention precious time for the forests to regenerate. To date, 100,000 women have created these tree-planting collectives, and one tree has become 40 million strong.

In Rwanda, after the utter decimation of the genocide, the women took control to rebuild their society. Bruised and beaten, raped and destroyed, women slowly began to pick up the pieces, leading the way to a newly forged nation of more equal rights and status. Now they are cabinet members and store owners, day labourers and policewomen, rewriting the laws and the history of a small war-torn country that almost caved in on itself in 1994. Rwanda has gone from an annihilated culture to a model for allowing women to take leadership roles and letting them lead the reconciliation of a nation.

In South Africa, women were crucial to the Truth and Reconciliation Commission that pulled the country from the evil depths of apartheid into a modern era of evolving potential. Through their brave testimony and facilitation of the reconciliation process, women have ushered in an era of progress that should serve as an example for other nations in strife, from Iraq to Darfur and from Burma to Lebanon.

Kiva.org and Grameen Bank are two examples of how microfinance has reengineered the possibilities for growth when women are allowed to empower themselves. Given tiny loans, not only do women almost always pay back the loan, but they also invest the money back into their communities and can often make extraordinary progress from just a few dollars. They are likely to send their children to school, wearing shoes and carrying pencils. All we need to do is make sure that schools are available to them, especially the little girls. All around the world, women are now entering the highest echelons of their trades and changing them for the better.

Greg Mortenson recognised the power of educating women; he moved mountains, starting with hiring local workers to build schools for girls in Pakistan and Afghanistan. As soon as the doors were open, there were smiling faces to greet them – the faces of future leaders. If we build a structure to house their dreams, girls will come to realise them, along with the dreams of their children, husbands, brothers and fathers.

Secretary of State Clinton recently spoke to the UN regarding the essential role of women's empowerment for US security, as well as other issues discussed here. Nicholas Kristof reiterated this fact in the *New York Times*, and has been a shedder of light on women's issues for many years.

Not every aspect is rose-colored. The demands of modern society place even more burdens on the women who already feed and raise their families while doing the lion's share of domestic work. A woman is supposed to remain beautiful, strong, disciplined, kind and polite while she completes the countless tasks that begin with each breaking dawn. We must fight not only for women's voices, but also for lives full of safe and dignified opportunities and protection for her spirit and mind.

Fathers, husbands and sons must be nurtured too, educated in the value of equality between the genders and given the same chance to thrive in the paternal role of hands-on father, hardworking student, proud worker and loving husband.

It is logical that a person intricately involved in the agricultural maintenance of a community should take part in its leadership; yet this disparity, forged in stereotypes, has prohibited women's advancement. It has also stunted her country's growth as a whole, because the most skilled individuals in terms of environmental sensitivities and natural expertise in diplomacy have been historically banned from the boardrooms and the decision-making processes.

If we can protect them from abuse and guide them to their own paths, women will lead the way for the rest of us to follow them to a more peaceful and prosperous future, especially in those countries still struggling with so much poverty and war.

What if I told you that I knew who held the key to a future free from the torture of hunger, the lack of schooling, the isolation of discrimination, the grief of infant death, the confusion of sparse pre-natal care, the agony of disease, the devastation of environmental degradation and the injustice in the developing world?

What if I told you that it was your daughter?

THIRD PLACE – ADULT

Margaret Casserly
Sligo, Ireland

MDG 3 – PROMOTE GENDER EQUALITY AND EMPOWER WOMEN

Mr. President, Mr. Secretary-General, Ladies and Gentlemen,

I am honoured to be here addressing you. You are familiar with experts addressing you as well as eminent people from every walk of life, but I am here as an ordinary citizen, you could say an 'Everyman', or in this case an 'Everywoman'. I sense the heavy weight on your shoulders, the weight of responsibility for all those of our fellow men, women and children who live in conditions which are unworthy of the twenty-first century. It is for all these, all our brothers and sisters on the planet, that the Millennium Development Goals have been drawn up. How can we best make progress?

I have chosen to focus on Millennium Development Goal number 3: Promote gender equality and empower women. Why? You may well ask. Why should this goal be chosen before that of poverty and hunger, maternal health, diseases and full primary education, global co-operation and sustainable living? All of these other goals are most worthy and each one deserves our attention. However, I put it to you today that women are the key to real progress.

I hasten to assure you that I am not some kind of zealot. No, my contention is simply this: women and men are equal and should be able to share equally in the decisions and responsibilities affecting their lives and that of their families.

As this is so self-evident, why do we need to promote the cause of women? It is a sad fact that many societies are still patriarchal to an extreme extent, allowing little freedom and autonomy to women, with the position of women very under-valued. Women may still be regarded as the property of their husband in some cultures. Their lives are mapped out for them, from scant education to early marriage to repeated pregnancies. They have very little choice in life; many suffer inhuman workloads, disrespect and even abuse. And yet women constitute half the human race; they have huge potential to contribute to society even apart from their fundamental role of motherhood.

But we have invested billions to date with ever worsening crises, I hear you say. Wars and political instability have been endemic. Yet how often have women instigated war? Why is the pursuit of power happening at the expense of the most vulnerable?

Many women are powerless. Without supportive laws and economic means of their own, women cannot have any independent decision making. They cannot leave abusive situations. They have no autonomy even within their own families. Pregnancy follows pregnancy with the ever present dangers of maternal mortality. Child mortality goes hand in hand with high birth rates; with extra mouths to feed, poverty becomes even greater and availing of education becomes an impossible dream. In countries where such poverty exists, universal health services cannot develop to combat infections, or to promote child and maternal health. Resources are exploited rather than developed in a sustainable way and global partnerships for development become the stuff of dreams.

Again, I assert that all the other Millennium Development Goals hinge on this most important one, number 3: Promote gender equality and empower women.

"This task is daunting; how can this be done?" you may ask. The answer is simple: Enact laws that ensure that women are given equal status. Ensure that these laws are enforced. Men must respect women and vice versa. This can be accomplished by the stroke of a pen but it must be followed up; equal rights must be enforced. This can be done by 2015. *You* can do it. *You* are leaders in your own countries. Now is the time to stand up for women's rights.

Empowerment of women will ensure equal access to education; women will be allowed to plan their families and their health; women will become able to earn comparable wages. Many may choose to earn small amounts to supplement the family income while continuing in their primary care-giving roles. Many will be enabled to avail of micro-loans to lift themselves out of poverty.

To illustrate this point, let us look at the practical empowerment of women via micro-credit as developed by Grameen Bank. Its founder, Professor Yunus, received the Nobel Prize in 2006. (You would think this was a large enough hint to the entire world, yet it seems we didn't quite get it).

Grameen credit is based on the fundamental idea that charity is not the answer to poverty; that respect and trust for the resilience and skills of poor people will break the cycle of dependency. Professor Yunus chose to lend to women first and the results were astounding. If this philosophy had prevailed, we would not have had the economic problems and recessions of the developed world either. The problem with capitalism, Yunus says, is its distinction between companies pursuing profit and charities pursuing good. His bank model operates with corporate efficiency, but pumps profits back into social objectives.

In many countries, women barter or sell their own produce to earn a little money. However, such food-related enterprises are being regulated out of existence. Bureaucracy may have lofty aims, but it can stifle enterprise. Along with access to a little start-up cash, it is important not to be over-regulated for people who operate on such a small scale. As leaders in your countries, this is another action you can take: to ensure that rules do not stifle micro enterprises while having sensible safeguards on health.

If a woman has access to a little money she will prioritise: her children will be fed first, not last. She will be more likely to save for their education than to invest in the local brew. She may be enabled to avail of adult education and primary health care initiatives because she is no longer in mere survival mode. Her self-respect will grow and this will spill over into her family rearing practices. Boys will see their mothers as people who deserve respect and in turn will look be respectful to their own partners. Girls will want to emulate their strong and caring mothers. It will take more than one generation for the full effects to show, but it can be done.

Alongside the enactment and enforcement of equal rights, it is vital to have a community development approach, with education in best practices of health, farming and sustainable living. It is a truism that clean water is more important that the most up to date hospital. Already in many countries, education about clean water supplies and simple fluid replacement has had a huge effect on the under-fives mortality rate from diarrhoea; simple immunisation programmes have been immensely successful. Mosquito nets are saving lives. These are not earth-shattering innovations but they are profoundly life-changing for those concerned. When child mortality drops, the fertility rate drops some years later. This phenomenon has been repeatedly demonstrated. Women no longer become baby factories, in the hope that a few will survive into adulthood and support their parents. Mothers can assume a more nurturing and educative role in their families. Families may be able to withstand the calamities thrown at them by life, with the strong maternal presence at the core. We also need more women in public office and parliaments. Equal status is key to all this.

Some examples will illustrate what progress can be achieved. First, one person's story: Waris Dirie, the Somalian model, embodies what may be achieved when women can choose. Fleeing from an arranged marriage at age 13, she became independent, having been sheltered by sympathetic women and enabled to earn for herself. Unexpected doors opened to her; she eventually told the story of her female genital mutilation as a three year old; now she acts to bring human rights to her African sisters.

We have a national story of progress from Mozambique where in 2005 legislators signed a new law that redefined the status of women as equal, including rights to property. Marriage laws were overhauled. Women are enabled to work outside the home without needing permission. This far-reaching legislation may be hard-won but it was a worthwhile battle.

So, as Everywoman, I appeal to you to take this simple and profound action: ensure the equality of women in every society. We are not talking of developing nations solely here; this also applies to many so-called 'developed' countries where women may still have a second-class status. Disempowerment is too insidious; it can negatively affect decisions and lives even of well educated girls. Boys and men need to understand that this does not mean a loss to their own status and traditions; quite the contrary. We are all stronger when each is respected and respectful. Together we do it better. Together we can achieve the Millennium Development Goals. Let us prioritise number 3: Promote gender equality and empower women.

The future belongs to us all – both women *and* men. *You* have the power to make it happen.

SHORTLIST – ADULT

Brian Harding

Dublin, Ireland

MDG 7 – ENSURE ENVIRONMENTAL SUSTAINABILITY

Mr. President, Mr. Secretary-General, Ladies and Gentlemen,

The world rests on a precipice and our world rests on your shoulders. Today, you gather here as the chief representative for your country but when we all come together like this, we stand together as a global family with common goals and aspirations. We acknowledge our differences but understand the importance of such gatherings. Our differences are not what drive us into these rooms but our common humanity. Everyone here shares similarities.

Our similarities are not just born of politics or governance. Our similarities start much earlier. All the way from childhood, we dream of change. We remember our childhoods because it shapes the men and women that we become. We remember play, adventures, tastes, touch and smells of the past, that live with us forever. As you look around this room, believe me when I tell you, you have all had a common experience together. I know all of you have felt connected to nature at some point in your life. From every corner of this planet human beings are intrinsically connected to the world around them – to their environment. Common bonds such as these are rare in humanity and hard to quantify – but I say just because you can't always count it, doesn't mean you can't value it. Children dream and create fantasy around the worlds that they live in – both imaginary and real.

They meander through the forests of their minds and alongside the rivers of their intellect as they seek out better ways to perceive the world that they live in. We require you to do the same. We require you to be true visionaries. To paraphrase the words of George Bernard Shaw: "Some see things as they are and ask why. Others dream things that never were and ask why not."

I am asking you to dream of another way to protect our planet. I am asking you to come together to find new unseen visions. I am asking you to find new directions and motivations. I am asking you to find commonality of cause. I am asking you to fight even harder to achieve the Millennium Development Goals and I'm asking you to especially focus on MDG 7, upon which all the others depend.

MDG 7 requires that everyone, especially governments, review the way we protect the world that we live in. Our greatest global resource is ourselves and our role is one of guardianship of the Earth's treasures. Humans do not always live in balance with their surroundings. We have strange connections with property and possessions, unlike many of our biological neighbours. We all have different perceptions of what we need to have a good life. We like shiny things. We like new things. We covet things that will not come with us after we pass on. Yet this does not stop us fighting for what we perceive to be our own. We can take none of it with us, yet we are misguided in believing that what we own is what defines our status and wealth, from individuals all the way to nation states. We want this generation to be the first that changes how we think as a human family, what it is that we actually "own" and what will we do to ensure that our children and our grandchildren are safe. We want you to lead.

The World Bank believes that three of the world's greatest challenges over the coming decades will be biodiversity loss, climate change and water shortages. All of these detrimental effects fit uncomfortably within MDG 7.

The world needs to you to tap into the true essence of our connection with our natural world – our biophilia. From the forests of Indonesia, to the bamboo stand of Sichuan, through the great savannahs of Africa and immersed amongst the seas off the Japanese coast, important keystones species are threatened by our unsustainable practices every day. All of our greatest resources reside within one of your territories. They do not belong to you. You are the global guardians of them. Feel free to conserve them, even to make money from protecting them, but just make sure when you leave this planet, they are safe. We must admit that we have not been doing well at protecting all life on our planet but like Oliver Goldsmith once declared: "Our greatest glory is not in never falling, but in rising every time we fall." We have fallen and faltered many times when it comes to protecting our world's biodiversity and with it we jeopardise the potential unfound cures that are to be found within the leaves, stems and roots of plants; we place ecosystems at risk that protect us from natural disasters like landslides, tsunamis, and even hurricanes and we take away one of the greatest barriers for protecting our atmosphere.

I often imagine life on this planet to be like the millions of stars that light up our night sky. Imagine every night one disappeared. Imagine we found out we were the cause. Would we do something? Would we simply watch as it got darker and darker? As global species disappear, will you stand idly by, and watch not as the light goes out, but life itself?

Did you know the Amazon is drying up? That glaciers are melting at alarming rates? Of course you do. We all know that the climate is changing. Climate change is a fact and is the greatest global challenge that mankind has ever faced. The scientific consensus has been built and scientific minds have backed the data. Oh yes, there have been mistakes, but who amongst us can say that we haven't made mistakes? We wanted to play our own game and the earth is shifting the posts. Sceptical minds don't want to believe what we have done. We should all be embarrassed – some more than others.

But as we damage our atmosphere irreparably, where have you all been?

Climate change affects all of us. Women and children, especially in the developing world, are affected even more. Climate change makes us think about our economies, "growth", our populations, wealth distributions, our food and in essence our humanity. Those of you who lead in developing nations will have seen the impacts more directly, as arid lands become even drier, as pastoralists bring their cattle to urban centres in search of water, as planting seasons change, as predicted rains either don't arrive or come unexpectedly, and as you notice declines in agricultural production. So now what do we do? Well, we must begin to mitigate the effects and we must adapt to the changing conditions. We all have a role to play. What technologies will assist, who will produce them and who will pay for it? Who will finance adaptation in the developing world? What will replace the Kyoto Protocol? As I watched you all gather in Copenhagen, with rally cries from all around the world ringing in your ears to find an equitable climate change deal, you disappointingly allowed vested interests and hegemony to dictate the proceedings. You failed. You must do better next time.

Finally, our world's fresh water is so unbelievably stressed that it fuels conflict and is a weapon at which many of you have held over your neighbours. No country should be fighting over natural resources, especially water. Our rivers and lakes run across and even demarcate our boundaries yet they are fundamentally common to us all. We must find ways to share them. Just like children learn to compromise at an early age, we too must always do the same when it comes to water. Just as our rivers traverse our many countries, we must cover as much ground in ensuring that all of the world's citizens have access to clean and safe quality drinking water. Water should be a unifying force for mankind and you its voice. Drink water, love water, teach water conservation, never war over water, and let it bring groups together to discuss its use. Water should be a catalyst for discussion, possibly even peace.

So what will you do? Can you find ways to ensure the polluter pays? Can you protect our biodiversity? Can you reduce the amount of time making decisions, reuse the exceptional talents that exist within your borders, recycle policies that have worked, and dump those that are holding us back from achieving a more sustainable planet? Will you make environment more important in your national budgets? Can you think of better ways to produce food? Will you revise our urban environments? Will you encourage your citizens to cycle and be healthy? Can you build parks, green spaces, cities that revolutionise how we think and feel? Can you find ways to send more oxygen into our atmosphere and keep carbon where it belongs? Will you be leaders, not just in name only? Believe in MDG 7, fight harder to achieve it and our global family will all benefit.

SHORTLIST – ADULT

Ndifor Elves Funnui

Zinder, Niger

MDG 4 – REDUCE CHILD MORTALITY

The Secretary-General of the United Nations, Heads of State and Governments, Ladies and Gentlemen, I greet you all.

About a decade ago, world leaders met and decided to end world poverty by 2015 and they set eight goals to meet these objectives. When we look closely at the progress made so far to achieve this objective, we notice that much has been done here and there but more is still left to be done. We could symbolise it as a half empty glass or half full glass depending on which side of the road you find yourself. As concerns progress in some of the eight goals, it has so far been like that of a chameleon. Of the eight goals set to end world poverty by 2015, the reduction of child mortality is the one that touches my heart greatly but it is sad that many children born especially in developing countries when these goals were set died before being able to see if the objectives were attained or not. I will beg with you to look at the half empty part of the glass as concerns this particular goal.

The reduction of child mortality still has a long way to go especially in developing countries and if this goal has to be attained, the United Nations has to take full leadership in every member countries. In many countries worldwide, the United Nations seems to be missing in action. They spend more time on the protocol side of activities and at times are dragged into national politics instead of them standing out firmly to guide governments in the right direction in the interest of their populations. The U.N has to take more leadership actions in the field so that fewer children die.

Corruption, bad governance and manipulated data are a hindrance to children attaining adulthood especially in developing countries. Members of governments spend more time thinking how they are going to fill their private bank accounts instead of supplying their health institutions with drugs necessary for the welfare of their children. Data are always manipulated to camouflage the real situation and children die unnoticed. Good governance and democracy have to be encouraged. As world leaders, you all have to take our responsibilities and address these issues for child mortality to be reduced.

We all know that to reduce child mortality, the environment in which these children are born and where they live has to be secure. When we take a look at the world today, we see that children are born in unsecured environments; insecurity caused both by humans and nature. There are wars going on in every corner of the world and innocent children are killed, landmines are left behind after conflicts, hospitals are destroyed by warring parties, health agents are forced to abandon their health centres, children are orphaned etc... Children in Iraq, Afghanistan and Somalia know what I mean. As if this is not enough, Mother Nature sends tsunamis and earthquakes to end the lives of children like were the cases in Asia and Haiti. How do we hope to reduce child mortality when our actions are a hindrance to this objective? As world leaders, I would like to call on you to always put diplomacy first; war is not always the best way out. We also have to fight climate change.

Studies have shown that a vast majority of children spend most of their time with their mothers and studies also show that literacy rates among women still remains very low especially in developing countries. Many women have never had basic education for one reason or the other. They lack basic knowledge on childcare not to talk of healthcare. Prenatal and postnatal care, exclusive breastfeeding, family planning and women's empowerment have to be reinforced so that women are empowered with enough knowledge to reduce child mortality. Women remain the first actor in the reduction of child mortality and unless they are armed with basic knowledge and decision-making, the reduction of child mortality shall never be achieved even after 2015.

In recent months, world populations have been facing the problem of high prices of basic necessities like food. Given that a majority of people in developing countries live on less than a dollar a day, food prices push them to concentrate on how to fill their stomachs and there is no talk of diversifying food intake or seeking medical care thereby opening the doors for malnutrition. Children are always the first victims in such situations. Children in this part of the world are generally born with low weights and their living conditions make things worse. If we want to reduce child mortality, we will have to see to it that these children have diversified meals on their tables. We can do this by investing on agriculture, capacity-building farmers on modern farming techniques, giving subvention to farmers in developing countries so that these countries can be autonomous food wise, cut down taxes on food products as well as sensitise rural populations on the importance of consuming diversified meals. Some NGOs are already doing this but they need more means and support from world leaders.

In sub-Sahara Africa, malaria remains a major cause of death among children. Though this disease can be prevented and treated, figures shamefully show what havoc it causes among children especially those below five years old. Treated mosquito nets remain a good method of prevention but these nets are hardly available for vulnerable populations because they are expensive. Treated mosquito nets leave donors destined to be given free of charge to vulnerable populations but corrupt governments decide to sell them to their populations. UNICEF knows something about this. Poverty pushes some families to sell theirs when they receive one free of charge. There is also the problem of expensive essential malaria drugs. In sub-Sahara Africa, given the rate of poverty, sick children are left to die of malaria because malaria drugs still remain shamefully expensive or they are treated with drugs bought from unqualified pharmacists on the roadside. I would like to call on the international community to make essential malaria drugs available at low cost so that everyone can be able to buy them. I would also like to call on pharmaceutical companies to put the lives of populations at the forefront of their activities rather than financial benefits. This will greatly cut down the number of children that die for lack of access to basic healthcare.

The lack of access to sanitary services still remains a hindrance to the reduction of child mortality. Studies have shown that some 2.5 billion people (especially in developing countries) live without improved sanitation and this figure is increasing. We cannot talk of reducing child mortality when these children do not have access to sanitary services. The number of health facilities does not meet population needs.

Access to drinking water still remains a dream; there are whole communities with no toilet facilities – people defecate in the open air leading to the spread of diseases; the number of trained health personnel is far below population needs and when there are health facilities, populations do not have transport means to get there. We have to invest in sanitation infrastructure, train more health personnel, construct more roads and rich nations should avoid hiring the few qualified health personnel that poor nations have. We should also invest in vaccinations campaigns in rural areas. We all know how far vaccinations (measles, meningitis, poliomyelitis etc.) can save children's lives.

I would like to call on rich nations and governments to dip their hands deeper into their pockets in order help poor nations. I appreciate all you have done so far but a lot still remains to be done. In my opinion, your aid will be more efficient if it does not pass through governments. Experience has shown that aid is better managed when it is given through international non-governmental organisations (INGO). Many governments are so corrupt that they never direct aids they receive towards vulnerable populations. These aids are directed towards private bank accounts in western countries. INGOs remain the best means of channelling aid towards vulnerable populations because they have better management capacity. If all the aid you give do not get to the designated populations, do not expect to reduce child mortality.

I would like to end by saying that reducing child mortality is just one of the eight millennium development goals and if the other goals are not achieved, the reduction of child mortality shall never be achieved and more and more children shall keep on dying before they celebrate their fifth anniversary. It is the responsibility of everyone to contribute in whatever means in the achievement of these goals and the United Nations Organisation and governments have to be more proactive so that children born today shall still be alive in 2015 to see how far we have gone with the achievement of these goals.

SHORTLIST – ADULT

Joanna John
Atlanta, Georgia, USA

MDG 1 – ERADICATE EXTREME POVERTY AND HUNGER

Mr. President, Mr. Secretary-General, Ladies and Gentlemen, I stand before you today in awe and extremely humbled to be granted this opportunity to address the world's most powerful organization, an organization that is known for its ability to resolve global issues.

I was so overwhelmed by excitement this morning that I found myself unable to consume my usual breakfast of toasted bagel with cream cheese and orange juice, and instead opted for a cup of black coffee. Ladies and gentlemen, not eating breakfast was my decision, but at that moment approximately 800 million people around the world did not have that choice.

Every year you as global leaders, as well as multinational governments and private entities, tally and provide statistics, all in the hopes of solving the ever-present issue of hunger but yet the problem still exists. Therefore, in order to put our mind at ease for still not having found the magic formula, myths are created and accepted as truth. As per www.worldhunger.org, one of the greatest myths is that there is not enough food available worldwide, but it is the price of food rather than its availability which is the real problem.

Therefore the hungry, who are usually the ones trapped in severe poverty, are unable to buy food, which leads to malnutrition. Eventually malnourishment leads to the inability to work in order to obtain money to pay for the food they need so badly. It is a vicious and never ending cycle. It has been noted that for every one per cent increase in the price of staple foods, 16 million people go hungry, and approximately 25,000 people die every day of hunger or hunger-related causes according to your own research. This is more than AIDS, malaria and tuberculosis combined.

Hunger is non-discriminatory. There is no nation, gender, race or age group that it does not favour. Television, radio and glossy magazine ads show faces of desperate and solemn faces of Latin American, Asian and African children. These are not isolated cases. In fact, within only a few minutes drive from this building, there are District of Columbia residents who are facing food insecurity. One out of six elderly people in the United States, the world's richest and most powerful nation, has an inadequate diet, while one out of every eight children under the age of twelve goes to bed hungry each night.

At this point you may be asking yourself, why is she here today? I am not a celebrity or a politician, but what I am is a concerned citizen who has made the decision that I too can become a participant in this fight against hunger, not by quoting statistics, as any literate individual who has access to the worldwide web can do that, but to plead with you to take a more proactive stance.

Mr. Treki, the United Nations General Assembly has made an excellent decision by electing you as President. Libya has been proactive in achieving its goals of eradicating extreme poverty and hunger and providing subsidies in health agriculture and food imports for its own people. It donated $500,000 worth of corn for hunger relief in Zambia in 2006, and is making concerted efforts to ensure that food is distributed to affected regions. But your most notable contribution is the Great Man-Made River, which has vastly increased the amount of arable land in your country.

At the 2002 Monterrey conference, and again at the 2002 Johannesburg summit, 22 countries honoured an agreement to make concrete efforts towards giving 0.7 per cent of our national income in aid to poor countries. Some of you have already reached your goal and I commend you. But to those who have not yet reached your goal, I plead with you to do the best you can as the resulting $195 billion will be enough to effectively end hunger and extreme poverty in the world. Hopefully, though the financial assistance you provide will include more than just the provision of food but also to help establish programs similar to the "food for work" and "food for education" programs, which create more independent and self-sustained nations.

But first and foremost, we must start by reducing hunger, if not totally eliminating it, within our own borders before we can solve hunger on a global scale. In Atlanta, Georgia, I watch tourists and locals alike walk idly by as the homeless shove tins and caps in their way, hoping to get enough change for a meal or at least a warm beverage to curb the pangs of hunger. And as I touched on earlier, right here in Washington D.C., one in eight District households is struggling against hunger and facing food insecurity. And in places such as Plano and Frisco in Texas, middle-class residents are now going hungry due to the recent recession and turning to local food banks and family services for the first time in their lives.

As I conclude, I will like for you to consider some interesting facts as noted by www.worldhunger.org. For the price of ten stealth bombers, 100 million deaths can be prevented. And for the price of one missile, a school full of children can eat lunch every day for five years. Mr. President, I am confident that you and your delegates can do so much more to end world hunger. Of course it is easy to make excuses and maybe even blame each other for what is not being done, but take heed – since I began reading this essay over 200 people have died of starvation. Thank You.

SHORTLIST – ADULT

Thandazile Mpofu

Harare, Zimbabwe

MDG 1 – ERADICATE EXTREME POVERTY AND HUNGER

Mr. President, Mr. Secretary-General, Ladies and Gentlemen,

Eugene Linden's "Winds of change are blowing" again. From out of the spirit of benevolent kinship, zephyrs arose some years back and developed with purpose. Unlike in the past, these winds are blowing for all mankind and their change will be felt everywhere.

The Millennium Development Goals (MDGs) are the compelling force that is sweeping across the globe and causing a significant shift. Of particular note are the differences that have been evidenced as a result of the pursuance of the poverty eradication goal. Commendable progress has been made to erode this condition of deprivation, specifically in China and India. In my view, the goal to eradicate extreme poverty and hunger is the most central.

The state of being poor has a baneful cause-and-effect link to other problems faced by humanity. By tackling this problem, simultaneous strides will be made to positively affect other areas such as reduction of hunger, achieving universal primary education or improving maternal health. Thus, with the aforementioned in mind, I urge world leaders to make the eradication of extreme poverty and hunger priority and to use the five years remaining to the 2015 MDGs deadline to ensure its total annihilation.

The winds of change must blow hardest against this dehumanising condition in order to eventually erode it away.

I am sure that world leaders have engaged many experts and professionals to discover effective ways in which they can tackle poverty in their countries. It is hoped that the suggestions I am going to put forward will make a small but useful contribution to this end. They are based on the need to give impetus to ongoing efforts.

Just as every journey begins with a single step, this undertaking requires focus on a single measurable indicator or poverty attack drive. My first idea involves each government selecting just one of the measurable indicators listed under the goal to eradicate poverty. Obviously this selection will be informed by careful consideration of unique national circumstances and wide consultation. The chosen indicator will then be translated into an objective for the country to work towards, through a national poverty eradication programme. This programme must be both extensive and intensive.

All too often, human development issues are perceived as being only the concern of certain entities in society like churches and non-governmental organisations. The extensiveness of the programme should therefore have the involvement of as many citizens as possible. It must be truly national. With regards its intensity, mechanisms must be put in place to ensure that it maintains the continued interest and participation of the populous.

Consequently, the timeframe during which the programme will run is key in order that it does not lose momentum. The type of national poverty alleviation programmes I envision are employment creation and skills training drives done on a large scale, having the same level of awareness, enthusiasm and involvement as pop idols. They will have effective impact to push the country in the right direction with regards the eradication of poverty and hunger. The programmes will be the gust of wind across nations that will result in global changes.

A crucial weapon in the fight against poverty and hunger is enabling people to make a living to support themselves and their dependants. Hence achieving employment for women, men and young people is distinctly stated as a target of the MDGs. Varying schools of thought exist, each prescribing the best way in which to stimulate employment in order to realise optimum economic gains. In this regard, I say to world leaders, "each to his own", provided that the route followed spares our fellow-man from resorting to the many forms of survival that rob people of their dignity. I also ask world leaders to consider another of my suggestions. This involves reprioritising their national job creation policies and programmes and giving precedence to self-employment or entrepreneurship endeavours. Statistics show that the degree of economic growth a country enjoys has a positive relation to the entrepreneurial activity there. This makes a compelling argument for governmental support of entrepreneurship. Additional benefits for the country are that entrepreneurs provide jobs, introduce innovation and stimulate economic growth.

On an individual level, one only has to speak to a successful business person to know the advantages to be obtained. Entrepreneurship could be the windfall that many countries need. Thus, with so much to gain, governments should make renewed efforts to achieve the employment targets set under the poverty eradication goal using programmes that assist entrepreneurs. Depending on the extent to which such programmes are already implemented, there will be need to redeploy resources to support budding business people and the systems that aid them. Adjustments in the education sector could also be required as is the need to instil a new mindset in society that makes them job-creators as opposed to job-seekers. However, I believe the financial and other costs of entrepreneurial programmes are worth the benefits; the greatest of which is having empowered and satisfied citizens.

The world economic crisis of recent years is being sited as a challenge that has and will continue to hinder progress towards the attainment of the MDGs. Fortunately, several countries and organisations have opted to use the crisis as an opportunity to rethink the MDG approach to development policy. With the future of this planet and its peoples largely in the hands of *you*, our world leaders, it is pivotal that a positive attitude to dealing with the world economic crisis prevails. After all, the wind does not stop blowing when it encounters a wall in its path. As such, means must be found to draw from the outcomes of the crisis. Subsequent creation or amendments to relevant policies and strategies will be done and ultimately the MDGs achieved.

Within the turmoil that was experienced in global markets lies a possible launch pad towards attaining the poverty eradication goal. This does not necessarily mean a radical departure from the norm. The strong public outcries that resulted from the crisis and were directed at large irresponsible corporations could be become the foundation of government-led social campaigns that are tied to MDG initiatives. These would be less aggressive drives that utilise an emotive tone to persuade citizens to action, such vigilant consumer protection bodies.

Another idea on a larger scale could be the introduction of stricter regulations and monitoring of the operations of financial institutions to protect depositors' funds and life savings, and thus ensure that a significant portion of the populace is not once again plunged into near poverty overnight

At the very least these ideas will set the right attitude to dealing with the effects of the world economic crisis in relation to attaining the MDGs. However, with the input of economic experts governments could engineer policies and effective programmes to use the outcomes of the global crisis to their advantage. The point is not to use the crisis as an excuse for not relieving the world's poorest of their plight. Despite the tumultuous events, China and India have made commendable progress vis-à-vis their MDG achievement. It follows, therefore, that any determined effort from any country can do so too.

My final appeal is made on a personal level to all world leaders. *You* pledged in the Millennium Declaration and undertook the responsibility to spare no effort to free our fellow men, women and children from the abject and dehumanising conditions of extreme poverty. I therefore, urge every leader to reaffirm your commitment to these purposes and principles. Poverty exists in all countries for many reasons such as historical injustices, inadequate resources, poor governance and civil unrest. I appeal to you all to do your best and satisfy your conscious that your actions do not contribute directly or indirectly to any of the reasons behind poverty in your country or beyond. With your true commitment it can be said with certainty that poverty and hunger will be eradicated. This may not have occurred by the MDG 2015 deadline but inevitably, the aspirations of the Millennium Declaration will be reached as the winds will have changed the landscape for the better.

SHORTLIST – ADULT

Yvonne Campbell

Dublin, Ireland

MDG 1 – ERADICATE EXTREME POVERTY AND HUNGER

To everything there is a season and a time for every purpose under heaven. Presidents, Kings and Queens, Prime Ministers and distinguished guests, this is our time to act. This is our time to stamp out poverty and make it history. This is our time to end hunger and the withering injustice of famine.

Ten years ago, a group of statesmen, in this very building where we stand today, signed the Millennium Declaration. This momentous declaration set out eight goals that aim to address the world's greatest development challenges by 2015. The first of those goals was to cut in half the number of people in the developing world living on less than $1.00 a day by 2015. It sought to achieve full and productive employment and decent work for all and halve the proportion of people who suffer from hunger.

But ten years later, poverty is still not history. Ten years later, the life of a child in Ethiopia is still threatened by the scourge of famine. Ten years later, slum dwellers, who account for 1 billion of the world's urban population, die earlier, experience more hunger and disease, receive less education and have fewer job opportunities. Ten years later, there are 1.4 billion people living in extreme poverty despite the fact that we possess enough food to feed the world. And so we've come here today to say enough is enough.

Enough with aching stomachs and malnourished arms; enough with exposed ribs and rickety legs; enough with bulging eyes and over-sized heads: We have promised our peoples that we would put an end to such inhumanity and we promised we would do so in our lifetime by 2015.

We promised.

Ladies and gentlemen, how can we sleep at night knowing that half of humanity will go to bed hungry? How can we throw out unwanted food knowing that hunger rivals obesity as a global problem? How can we subsidise our agricultural sectors knowing that it impacts negatively on the very places to which we send food aid?

We promised.

So how can we begin to solve this problem? Well when others said we couldn't do it, we said "Yes we can". Microfinance has proven a useful tool for alleviating poverty in Bangladesh. Malawi has initiated a voucher programme for fertilizers and seeds which is helping to end hunger and related poverty. Using modern science, a new rice for Africa has been developed. This hybrid between the Asian and African rice is a high-yielding, drought resistant and protein-rich variety that has contributed to food security and improved nutrition in several countries on the continent. TNT and the World Food Programme called their partnership "Moving the World" and the UN views it as a success in the fight against global hunger.

We promised.

But more needs to be done. Emergency food aid and school feeding programmes are badly needed. There needs to be more research and development in yield-enhancing agricultural and climate change technologies. Partnerships must be forged between civil society and the private sector. Urban development projects must clear slums to enhance the quality of life of the poor. Social welfare systems need to be in place to act more as a springboard than a safety net to help people return to work and live productive lives. There must be equal access to economic resources and decent work.

Above all, there needs to be political will. We promised and we must make good our promises. Not only did we make the solemn promises in the Millennium Declaration, we set out concrete steps at the High-Level Conference on World Food Security in 2008. We must do what we say we will do. This is not rocket science. This is humanity or rather this is our inhumanity to our fellow men and women.

Change can happen for the good. Aid directed to basic education for low-income countries increased from $1.6billion in 1999 to $5 billion in 2006. In 2006, for the first time since mortality data has been gathered, annual deaths among children under five dropped below 10 million to 9.7 million. In Ghana, public school enrolment in the most deprived districts soared from 4.2 million to 5.4 million between 2004 and 2005.

We promised.

Look at the response to the devastating earthquake in Haiti. Within hours, the international community and civil society mobilised itself to deliver the necessary search and rescue facilities, aid supplies and reconstruction experts. It seems that where there is political will there is a way to get things done.

We promised.

Ladies and gentlemen, the time to act is now. Now, only five years away from the deadline, we must do all we can to realise the Millennium Development Goals. We must increase our Overseas Development Aid budgets to 0.7 per cent of GDP. We must fund those programmes which are best placed to realise the goals by 2015.

Failure to act now will perpetuate the heinous crime of a starving child, dying of malnutrition. Failure to act will intensify the fires of hate and anger that fuel terrorism and attacks on liberty. Failure to act will consign this institution, the United Nations, to the dustbin of history, to wither away with the Declaration that promised so much but delivered so little.

And so, ladies and gentlemen, we are faced with a choice. Do we redouble our efforts to meet the targets by 2015 or do we wait until 2015 to agree another 15 year plan? If we choose to wait we must know that the number of underweight children will continue to exceed 140 million. Women will continue to die of complications related to pregnancy and childbirth. Current estimates suggest that 500,000 die a year. If we wait until 2015, 2.5 million women will die; 2.5 million will be dead because we did not care enough. If recent increases in food prices continue, we could be facing 2 million undernourished and 1 billion hungry by 2015. If we wait the problems will get worse.

But there is hope. The United Nations believes the goal of halving poverty can be reached by 2015. Already, extraordinary progress has been made in East Asia and even in sub-Saharan Africa the poverty rate has remained constant at around 50 per cent. Higher quality jobs could help to lift more people out of poverty while greater investment in agriculture and rural markets could tackle the problem of hunger.

The world is not short of ideas. The world is not short of good intentions. The world is short, however, of political will. So Presidents, Kings and Queens, Prime Ministers and distinguished guests, summon the necessary political will and deliver upon your promises made at the opening of the new millennium. Summon the necessary energy to realise the goals and revel in the success of reaching the various targets. Summon the courage to change the systems that perpetuate inequality, poverty and hunger and rejoice in the "win-win" situation in which you will find yourselves.

Together, ladies and gentlemen, we can feed the world and let them know it's action time. Thank you.

SHORTLIST – ADULT

Elizabeth Doane
Boston, Massachusetts, USA

MDG 2 – ACHIEVE UNIVERSAL PRIMARY EDUCATION

Mr. President, Mr. Secretary-General, Ladies and Gentlemen,

Thank you for allowing me to address you here today. In the years since the Millennium Development Goals were first created, great strides have been made in the developing world. Infant mortality has declined, fewer mothers are dying during delivery, more children are attending schools, and the numbers of those living in extreme poverty have been reduced. But with just five years to go before the Millennium Development Goals are due to be met, there is still much work to be done to deliver on those promises.

In building these nations from the ground up, everyone in this room is an architect of development and each millennium goal is a brick. While every brick has importance and purpose, it is the foundation that determines the strength of a building. It is my belief that universal education is that foundation. We have drawn up the plans, and started the groundwork, but this is where the metaphor ends, for although we are here to begin building, it is up to the people of the developing world to finish construction. Is it not the eventual goal for each nation to continue building themselves? As any architect can tell you, a structure with a weak foundation will eventually fall, just as a country without an educated population will cease to develop. Therefore, if sustainability is the overarching goal, then education should be the priority, because, sustainability can only be reached through quality education for all. How else can the people be prepared to manage the challenges of modern governments?

Investments in education have been proven to have residual benefits across other sectors as well; therefore, if we deliver on universal primary education, we will be able to better deliver on the rest of the Millennium Goals. For example, a study conducted by the Global Campaign for Education concluded that if all children had a primary education, approximately 700,000 cases of HIV could be prevented every year. Combating HIV/AIDS, as you well know, is reflected in MDG 6. This dramatic decrease in the number of new infections could put us that must closer to halting the spread of HIV/AIDS worldwide without double counting expenditures.

Improvements in education can also help generate economic growth, which would aid in the reduction of world poverty, as expressed in MDG 1. In a 100-country study facilitated by the World Bank, researchers concluded that a one percent increase in the level of education, especially among women, stimulates 0.3 per cent in additional economic growth. This economic growth could create jobs, raise standards of living, and decrease world hunger as promised by several of the Millennium Development Goals. By allocating more money to universal primary education, benefits will be magnified across other crucial sectors.

It is true that the number of children in school has increased worldwide, especially at the primary level, and this is a great achievement. However, too often the focus remains on statistics and sheer numbers to determine the success of a program. It is important to not just address the quantity of children in school, but the quality of education that they are receiving. While ensuring attendance is clearly the first step, it is not enough to gather children in a classroom and claim them as a success story. Therefore I propose that we invest not only in getting children to school, but in the teachers and materials responsible for their education.

To illustrate this point, I wish to draw your attention to a personal experience I had in the West African nation of Niger. As one of the poorest countries in the world, Niger is struggling to feed its population, provide quality healthcare, and even maintain political stability. As a francophone nation, the school system teaches in French, although the vast majority of the population do not speak French at home, which is a problem in itself. In 2009, I spent four months in Niger, living with a family in a small neighbourhood outside of Niamey. As it was a polygamous Hausa family, I had twelve host brothers and sisters, nine of which were of schooling age. Of those nine, all of them were attending school. With the net enrolment rate in Niger hovering around 45 per cent, nine children attending school is a rarity that speaks wonders of my host family. However, I soon came to realize that attending school does not necessarily result in education.

One night after the children had returned from school, my sister Ramatu, who at age 14 was in her sixth year of school, asked me to help her with her homework. We sat down together, and she handed me her notebook, looking up at me expectantly. After expressing my confusion, she instructed me to read aloud the notes in French that she had taken in class that day. I handed the notebook back to her, and said that she should read the notes aloud to me instead. She shook her head and replied simply that she could not. I pointed to a word on the page, and although she had written everything in the notebook, she could not read single word she had written.

Still wanting to help, I began to read the notes aloud. The lesson that day had been on geography, specifically that of Niger. At the end of each phrase, Ramatu would repeat exactly what I had just read to her. As this continued, I began to realize that she did not understand what I was reading, nor what she was repeating. Curious, I asked her for definitions of several words in the lesson. I read the word Sahara aloud; she could not tell me what it was. I read the word ocean aloud; she could not tell me what it was. I read the word mountain aloud; she could not tell me what it was. How is it possible that in six years, my sister was not able to learn to read, or understand the French in her own classroom? It suddenly became clear to me that Ramatu was not learning information, but rather learning how to memorize phrases and parrot them back to her teacher. I assure you that this is no shortcoming of her own; these habits held true for all of my host siblings, and are not limited to this family, city, or country.

This, ladies and gentlemen, is not quality education, and quite frankly is not doing much good. It is a waste of time and money to allow this type of feeble education to continue. Every day, children desperate to learn are disappointed by the failures of the school system. This not only directly influences the children attending school, but undermines the very attendance that we have been striving for. What motivation do families have to send their children to school when they are not learning properly?

To combat these grave problems, more money needs to be allocated towards developing a professional staff of teachers who understand the enormity of their position. A teacher's influence has the potential to last a life-time, to instil in their pupils a curiosity and love of learning, a need to explore and create, to solve problems on their own. The cultivation of these characteristics is invaluable and, to return to the previous metaphor, will provide the necessary foundation to build these nations into a functioning state. It has been estimated that universal primary education would cost $10 billion a year; and although that sounds like a lot, that is half of what Americans will spend on ice cream in a given year. Speaking as an American, I would much rather give up ice cream in order to see children around the world reaching their full potential.

In a sense, the goal of development work is to render ourselves unnecessary; to not be needed anymore. But, as long as we fail to deliver on quality primary education, our presence will always be needed. As said by Nelson Mandela, "Education is the most powerful weapon which you can use to change the world."

Once we give the people of these nations that weapon, I'm sure there will be no stopping them from enormous achievement. Let us deliver on those promises we made, and give children everywhere the quality education they deserve.

SHORTLIST – ADULT

Sounmitra Subinaya

Orissa, India

MDG 3 – PROMOTE GENDER EQUALITY AND EMPOWER WOMEN

Mr. President, Mr. Secretary-General, Ladies and Gentlemen,

What can a woman do?

In 1928, a young Albanian woman arrived in a city in India where the destitute were dying hungry on the streets; the disabled were being abandoned; people from neighbouring countries kept on pouring into the city in large numbers to seek refuge; slums and diseases were growing hand in hand; the Hindus, the Muslims and the Christians were all at loggerheads with one another, and the society was highly patriarchal. She wanted to change this city of pain into a city of joy. But, "What could a lone woman with just three pennies in her pocket do?"

She could change the world.

This woman of substance was Mother Teresa. Mother was not only an Angel of Mercy but also an amazing institution builder and social entrepreneur. In 1950, she founded her order, the Missionaries of Charity, with only 12 nuns and today, the order operates with 4,540 sisters in 132 countries! This is the power of woman. A woman can change the world. Even the father of my nation, Mahatma Gandhi believed that women were the repositories of immense power and that women could be strong nation builders. The Nobel Laureate from my country, the late Rabindranath Tagore, wrote that "woman is the builder and moulder of a nation's destiny". However even today in the twenty-first century we underestimate a woman's potential and discriminate her. As a child in my small village in India, I saw my grandmother put two eggs on my food plate while my sister got one. When I asked her the reason, she told me that boys deserved more nutritious food than girls as boys grow up to be the bread earners of the family. She often described my sister as a burden on the family. I still remember the day when my sister was born. My mother was humiliated in front of the villagers for giving birth to a girl. I completed my schooling and went to the college but my sister was not allowed to complete her high school. She was asked to help my mother in cooking and cleaning the house. I saw how patriarchal and sexist my family members were. As I grew up, I noticed that not only my family members but the whole society around me was patriarchal and sexist. Though the constitution of my country guaranteed equal rights for men and women, several laws had a discriminatory colour against women. Amongst such laws were The Women's Right to Property Act, 1937 that gave rights to the widow to demand partition in the deceased husband's estate and to claim and possess properties equal to the share of her son. But it gave *no* such right to her daughter. The Hindu Succession Act, 1956 also gave only partial relief to the daughter. However, as of 2005, the Act has been amended and now the son and the daughter are equal coparceners in their parental property.

The case of Muslim women in my country is still deplorable. While monogamy is the rule for a Muslim wife, the husband is entitled to have four wives at a time. The husband can divorce his wife unilaterally without any fault or cause. If the husband becomes an apostate, it operates as dissolution of marriage but if the wife becomes an apostate, this will normally not occur.

A Muslim woman is not entitled to be the guardian of the property of her minor child. The rule in Muslim law of inheritance is that the share of a male heir of the same degree is twice that of a female. Thus, the share of a son is twice that of a daughter and that of a brother twice that of the sister of the same degree.

Further, Section 10 of the Indian Divorce Act, 1869, provides that the husband is entitled to obtain divorce on the ground of the wife's adultery. But the wife has to prove an aggravating circumstance in addition to adultery, such as apostasy or marriage with another woman by the husband.

This is not the case in my country only but laws similar to the above are prevalent in many developing nations around the world. I have seen women in my village being paid less than men even though both would have worked equally. Further, in the society I live in, a woman is criticised for doing a job. She is often physically and mentally tormented and is forced to remain within the four walls of the house. She is not allowed to gain independence financially. As a result she is always considered inferior to man who provides food and financial security to the entire family.

Today, I speak not only for the women in my country but for all women around the world. It is time to achieve the Millennium Development Goal number 3, which provides for gender equality and empowerment of woman. To achieve the same, I suggest women all around the world should not only be made literates but also legal-literates. They should be made aware of their fundamental rights and constitutional remedies when faced with discrimination. They should be assured that they are as equal human beings as their male counterparts are and both the genders have equal human rights. They should be provided with free legal aid. Even today, professions such as engineering, law and armed forces, navy and air force are male dominated. Recruiters believe that women are not suitable for such so-called "male jobs".

This mindset must go. To make women at par with men, they should be provided with ample employment opportunities.

Women self-help groups that have come up in many parts of South Asia are providing women with confidence and financial independence. With the aid of microcredit from banks women have been able to adopt entrepreneurial careers. Women can be empowered if laws that treat women unequally are repealed. The Property Laws, the Muslim personal law need to be amended so as to make them women-friendly. To promote compensatory justice, affirmative action should be undertaken all over the world and seats should be reserved for women at the national parliaments and state assemblies all over the world. Practices such as female infanticide, dowry, sati and child marriage should be checked. Positive discrimination policies for women providing quotas in educational institutions all over the world should be framed. All the countries should be persuaded to become signatories to CEDAW. Women should be given autonomy to choose their vocation and should be provided with adequate food and clothing.

I still remember my grandmother giving me two eggs and my sister just one. Such discrimination can only be destroyed with the aid of gender-sensitization programmes. I appeal to the presidents of all nations not only to educate their women about the women's rights but also educate men to treat women equally. Thus, I propose conducting workshops and gender sensitization programmes all over the world. Further, I appeal to the leaders present here to create special leadership programmes for rural women to enable them to come out of their households and become active citizens.

In this way, I am sure that we can together realise the Millennium Development Goal number 3 and create a world with gender equality and empowered women folk. I would like to conclude by repeating the words of the famous poet Nobel Laureate Tagore: "Woman is the builder and moulder of a nation's destiny. Though delicate and soft as a lily she has a heart far stronger and bolder than man – she is the supreme inspiration for man's onward march, an embodiment of love, pity and compassion."

PASSAGES/EXTRACTS/QUOTES – ADULT CATEGORY

Ibn Garba Safiya

Kaduna, Nigeria

MDG 3 – PROMOTE GENDER EQUALITY AND EMPOWER WOMEN

… I am here particularly because I believe that by promoting gender equality and empowering women we can achieve all of the millennium development goals. I am here because I believe in women and their potential to effect change for development.

Back home, we are struggling, struggling to feed our families, struggling to educate our children, struggling to reduce the unnecessary death of children and mothers, struggling to fight HIV/AIDS, malaria and other diseases, struggling to ensure our world doesn't give out on us and struggling to ensure that every land is developed and prosperous.

We are struggling because we need you to do more. Our best efforts can only do so much without your help; I am afraid that we will not meet these targets without your additional efforts and will.

Back home girls and women are still being discriminated against, don't get equal opportunities in education, in their careers and even in their homes. Many still roam our streets hawking, begging or getting into trouble.

I am asking you today to do more to ensure gender equity. Whether it is unwarranted killing of innocent citizens in the dead of the night or the inability of the political class to effectively sort themselves out present or absent, women are the ones who bear the brunt. I want you to imagine for a moment the agony of a woman who lost seven children to unwarranted war or the inability of a widow to feed her family because she wasn't given a chance to work. Every day back home women are abused, discriminated against, frustrated and ignored.

For how long will we sit back and sign agreements, make speeches and sound politically correct while women are denied even their basic rights. Shall we continue to attend meetings and conferences when in some countries like mine, 70 per cent of the population live below the poverty line and over 50 per cent of those people are women?

We only need to look at countries who have set good examples by empowering women by giving them opportunities as well to hold the reigns in governance and business and see where it has taken them.

I am here to ask you to do something and to do it urgently.

Nicholas Santizo

Manila, Philippines

MDG 2 – Achieve Universal Primary Education

... On my way to the airport, a young boy knocked on my car window with his palms held outward and his face in despair. He was asking for some food, and all I could spare him was a packed lunch I intended to eat while I was waiting for my flight. He gladly took my paper bag with a tempered enthusiasm borne out of years of hunger and begging... or stealing. His face showed the emotion of having to make do with this brown paper bag for now.

These are the kind of occurrences that happen every day in my home country, the Philippines. Young children are constantly forced into the streets, forced to fend for themselves and deprived of the opportunity to dream. For how could they dream if all they could think about was getting to their next meal? This left into me thinking as to why, despite all the promise that the Millennium Development Goals was able to cultivate for us, was nothing done for these children?

Of course, I am not here to merely pass judgement on our collective failures on humankind. After all, no good thing ever came out of pure negativity. There have been, of course, various levels of success on our different goals. Who could deny the progress we have made in lessening carbon emissions? Likewise, how can one not see the tremendous impact of globalization in our lives? I am, as of this moment, wearing a Filipino made Polo Barong, an American made pair of shoes and a Japanese made watch. All of these items could only have been made available to me by globalization and the thorough determination of our nations to peacefully cooperate and fairly trade with each other. But, suffice it to say, these achievements are still not enough.

For while there have been significant steps taken to alleviate the situation of our less fortunate brothers and sisters, it is still not enough. To the boy who begged to me on the streets of Manila, it is not enough. To every single soul out there that is hungry, cold and unhappy, due to no other reason but poverty, it is not enough. Indeed, so long as poverty exists, we shall have failed. Hence, we must continue to persevere, continue to struggle, for our real goal is not merely to halve poverty. It is to eliminate it completely. And just like the late Pres. Kennedy, I firmly believe that it is in our capacity to do so.

This brings me back to our goal of universal education. I believe that the real reason why the Millennium Development Goals on Universal Education did not succeed in the way we had hoped is because it put too much emphasis on building classrooms and creating legislation, rather than building relationships and empowering the disenfranchised. In other words, it put too much emphasis on having a good political agenda, rather making people care.

If Efren Peñaflorida, armed with just a push-cart classroom, could give street kids hope, why can't a worldwide alliance? If one man can convince thousands of street kids to stop sniffing rugby and to stop stealing, then why can't millions?

Efren was able to make a difference because he cared. He was able to make a difference, because it was he himself who went into these depressed areas and took the time to listen. He was able to make a difference because he had enough faith in these kids to teach them math and science believing fully that that these kids would make good use of their newfound knowledge to better their lives. This despite the fact that these are the kinds of kids who usually end up in gangs during their early teens only to die before they even reach the age of 30. These are the kinds of kids who usually get married at age 12 and bear 10 children simply because they do not know any better. These are the kinds of kids who are often ignored by society, and sometimes even forgotten.

This is why I propose that we make a significant change in focus. It is the only way for us to truly achieve our goal of eliminating poverty. First, let us get rid of our obtuse deadline of eliminating poverty by 2015. Poverty is simply too enduring and too difficult of an enemy to simply stamp an expiry date on. Instead, let us focus on achieving our specific goals one by one, and make deadlines as we go. Not only will it be more realistic, it will also sound less political and more humanitarian.

Secondly, let us shift our concentration from just trying to build classrooms and sound policies into trying to "build" people. Let us go to these depressed areas ourselves and show these forgotten people that we care. And maybe, just maybe, we'd get to know them a little bit better, and gain a newfound respect for them. It is said after all, that before you say anything about a person, you must first walk a mile in his shoes.

With that, let us encourage more people to reach out to them and start believing in them. They are our brothers and sisters after all, no matter how crude, how rude or unintelligent they may seem. Let us also train more teachers and social workers. For their contribution to society goes far beyond the dollar signs they may be able to produce for us. Their contribution to society, in reality, is priceless.

The real answer to poverty is not in having the best political agenda. It is not enough that 200 world leaders gather together to make an 8-point plan and throwing huge amounts of money into it. No amount of money or planning can eliminate poverty. The answer to poverty lies with the poor themselves. And the best way for the poor to help themselves is by arming them with education.

William Butler Yeats once said, "Education is not the filling of a bucket, it is the lighting of a fire." When we go into these depressed areas, we do not go there to stuff math and science into their heads. We go there to care and to show them that we believe in them. With that, I trust that they will educate themselves.

So let us, together, rediscover our faith in these people. Let us respect them and love them, as well as give them books to feed their minds and their imaginations. And together, let us watch them rise up to become a great ball of flame in the sky. Let us watch them become their own stars. For maybe the next time that we gather together to assess our success, it would be that boy who once begged for food in the streets of Manila who will be standing here in front of you and congratulating us all for our success. Just maybe ...

Dashell Yancha

Gothenberg, Sweden

MDG 7– ENSURE ENVIRONMENTAL SUSTAINABILITY

I have always been fascinated by the insights represented by the butterfly effect – a phrase coined by Edward Lorenz to refer to the idea that a butterfly's wings might create small changes in the atmosphere that could change the path, delay, accelerate or even prevent the occurrence of a tornado. The flapping of the wings of the butterfly represents small changes in the initial conditions of a system which might eventually cause a chain of events leading to large-scale transformation or if I may put it more radically, inspire a revolution. And so it is with the Millennium Development Goals or commonly known as the MDGs: the goals, when taken holistically, might seem rather arduous and herculean. Yet, breaking down these goals into their targets – likened to tiny flaps of the butterfly's wings – might possibly lead to large scale alterations in the state of world poverty and hunger, education, women empowerment, maternal health, child mortality, diseases, global partnership, and environmental sustainability. Small achievements in these targets could send tiny ripples that could create small tides of positive energy in the sea of global concerns. Hence a small flap in the area of world hunger could reverberate and leave a positive impact on global partnership and development.

Mr. President, Mr. Secretary-General, Ladies and Gentlemen, good evening.

The butterfly effect also stands for an important concept that is crucial in the achievement of the MDGs: interdependence. As the world becomes increasingly connected through the various modes facilitated by the processes of globalisation, we also become aware of our interdependence with the rest of the world. This is reflected in the way we conduct international relations: there are no longer domestic problems that do not have global implications; and national policy almost always impinges upon the conduct of foreign policy. States become mirrors of the world: poverty in one country reflects world hunger; in the same manner that increased maternal mortality exposes a general lack of empowerment among women.

Having reiterated this unmistakable interdependence of global problems as well as their solutions, I will now focus on one millennium goal which I think aptly represents this interdependence: goal number seven on ensuring environmental sustainability.

Let us, for one moment, stretch our imagination further and envision a seemingly close to utopic world where not only are there no lawyers but also that all the targets of the seven other goals have been achieved. By a stroke of some magical wand, the proportion of people living on less than $1 a day and those living in hunger had been halved; all children can have a complete course of primary education; gender disparity is eliminated; child mortality is reduced; universal access to reproductive health is achieved; the spread of HIV/AIDS and other diseases have been halted and have begun to reverse; and states have developed an open, rule-based, predictable, and non-discriminatory trading and financial system. Yet, and apologies for disrupting this vision of a seemingly perfect world, we wake up one day to realize that the earth can no longer sustain life. This may sound like some apocalyptic Hollywood movie conjured from strands of twisted imagination, but it could possibly happen. For like a human body that needs proper maintenance and care, the environment is susceptible to some form of death, where the vital parts, i.e. air, land, and water could just stop functioning – or malfunction in a way that can no longer sustain life on earth. And the level of global progress achieved through the elimination of world hunger, empowerment of women, reduction of child mortality, improvement of maternal health and achievement of all the other goals could be rendered meaningless.

But this is painting a rather naive scenario that defies logic, for we cannot achieve all the other goals without having a sustainable environment to achieve it in the first place. We cannot separate the end from the means of achieving our goals. The enabling condition that would allow us to realize all the other goals rests on ensuring a sustainable environment for its achievement.

The goal of ensuring a sustainable environment is woven interdependently with all the other goals. For instance, addressing world hunger also means taking into consideration that peoples' livelihoods and food security depend on a healthy and balanced ecosystem; access to universal primary education and achieving gender equality and women empowerment necessitates access to the right socio-economic infrastructure that is in harmony with environmental sustainability; the reduction of child mortality, the improvement of maternal health and the fight against HIV/AIDS, malaria and other diseases call for some basic environmentally-sound mechanisms such as access to clean water; and global partnership and development is made more meaningful if respect for the global commons is embodied in the national policies of states through environmental laws…

Meenakshi Roy

Roseville, Minnesota, USA

MDG 3 – PROMOTE GENDER EQUALITY AND EMPOWER WOMEN

... However, I do wonder about the alternatives for illiterate women to earn money to feed hungry mouths. Should we continue to build projects that utilize their vocational skills in urban homes (as domestic help) or in low-paying jobs like cooking or sewing, which do not offer job security or benefits? And if that be so, *are we then simply treating the symptoms rather than finding a cure?*

Now is the time to think. There is a global recognition that marginalized and battered women need to be helped. Multiple global projects exist, which provide vocational training, technical, administrative and logistical support to empower women and improve their footing as wage-earners. Undoubtedly, we are *doing things right*. This is of paramount importance. However, to truly maximize these initiatives, it is critical to *do the right thing*. Five years from now, do we want to continue helping uneducated women, or do we want to make sure there is no such child who grows up uneducated? Educating the girl child is the single-most effective panacea; the right thing to do.

I don't need to go over the statistics, do I? Two-thirds of the 300 million illiterate children of the world are girls. In my country India alone, the numbers are unnerving. Despite improvements in literacy rates over the past decade, significant gender disparities in education persist. Indian literacy rate of girls over 7 years of age is a staggering 33-50 per cent (differing from state to state), as against 75 per cent for boys. The self-proclaimed moral custodians of our medieval society continue to propagate dubious theories under the garb of ancient traditions and culture. Destitute parents actually believe they are saving their honour by marrying off their daughters early. There is a clear preference for sons for continuation of the clan and as bread-earners. Although several nations provide free primary education for all, the costs of books and uniforms often prove to be a deterrent. Cultural stereotypes subordinate the girl child by confining her to the narrow domestic sphere of the household, while the desperate ones end up selling their wombs or their bodies for money.

It is imperative to understand that education for girls usually improves their job opportunities and their quality of life. It is the single-most effective way to do away with such harmful practices and beliefs that continue to plague so many nations. Lack of education not merely precludes them from productive employment opportunities but also affects the quality of life. Women with education usually are financially, emotionally independent and have more decision-making power in their families. They are more likely to marry later in life (not in their teens), or have their first child later. The findings of the some global studies corroborate with the National Family Health Survey results in India - the association between maternal education and child mortality rates. All components of child mortality decline with increasing maternal education.

Significant work has been done to improve the girl child literacy rate. That notwithstanding, it is also abundantly clear that despite constitutional provisions on equal legal status for the girl child and the numerous enactments in its pursuance, there has been little progress. Undoubtedly, old traditions and cultures take time to change. Here is where we all can contribute. However much we may bewail the failure of legislative systems to provide protection to the girl child, the harsh reality is that unless change occurs in society's own "centuries old" gender discriminatory cultural biases, no governmental action can succeed by itself. It will only be possible through small projects at grass root levels. These projects will enable us to test different approaches in full collaboration with the community and families at large and learn important lessons to alleviate the problems thereof. There are numerous issues that call for new strategic paradigm shifts. How additional income-generating opportunities and better livelihood options could be made accessible, so that the girl child is allowed an education? How could awareness be built against gruesome practices of prenatal sex selection and feticide? How should families be made conscious of the importance of better healthcare, nutrition and education for the girl child? These are the kind of issues that the projects should deal with. These projects can start as a compulsory part of the curricula in urban schools and universities, so that the youth can be actively involved. Viable approaches from these projects can then be concretized. After independent evaluations of the methodologies adopted, techniques developed and lessons learnt, these field-tested measures could then be replicated on a larger scale. It could then be handed over for implementation to credible organizations that have the experience of working on similar issues.

All we need to do is to open our eyes. There are Sheelas and Pujas all around us. But we just don't care enough to see. Nor understand. And when we do, we rave and we rant. And in the end, we walk away, thanking our stars we weren't born as one of them. We are content to celebrate Women's day and wish each other every year. But hey, stop a moment. This is important.

Here I stand, a woman of the world, urging you to think.

As women we celebrate our independence today. But when will we be free?

SOUNDBITES – ADULT CATEGORY

Arvind Kumar Apsingikar

Hyderabad, India

MDG 2 – ACHIEVE UNIVERSAL PRIMARY EDUCATION

If the MDGs are to be realized there is a need to listen to the true voice of the poor. The true voice of any parent across the universe is that their children should not suffer like them and recognize strongly that Education is the only ultimate solution for their child's better quality of life.

Tara Finglas

Dublin, Ireland

MDG 8 – DEVELOP A GLOBAL PARTNERSHIP FOR DEVELOPMENT

Developing a Global Partnership for Development is an ongoing process and each one of you here today has the power and the foresight to see the writing on the wall. In five years time we will be here again but it is up to you to decide in what context. Will we be lamenting an opportunity lost to change the world or will we be in a new age of humanity? The choice is yours and the time is *now!*

Innocent Chidi Iskiakpu

Port Harcourt, Nigeria

MDG 3 – Promote Gender Equality and Empower Women

This is because poverty has a woman's face. It takes only a woman to understand what it means for a child to say "I am hungry." And any nation where women are empowered with a sense of responsibility as this, stand a much greater chance of achieving the millennium goals by 2015.

Cathy Howlett

Dublin, Ireland

MDG 5 – Improve Maternal Health

… How can this be happening in this day and age? In a time of globalization, industrialization and mass communication how is that hundreds of thousands of mothers die every year whilst partaking in the oldest and most natural rite in the world? Why is it that a girl like me can expect to give birth in safety and comfort, secure in the knowledge that any possible complications will be dealt with by a masterful hand? Yet a girl like Amma faces having what should be the most beauteous and awesome experience of her life tarnished by thoughts of all that could potentially go wrong. It seems unjust, wrong even that the wonder of life can be so closely linked to death – as if the beauty of one is dancing a relentless waltz with the horror of the other.

Mary Wall

Dublin, Ireland

MDG 2 – ACHIEVE UNIVERSAL PRIMARY EDUCATION

... Achieving Universal Primary Education may be just one of the 8 Goals in the UN Declaration, however each and every one of those Goals must be integrated and work in tandem and in parallel with the other. For example, the food programmes within the school system have a two-fold effect, encouraging the child to attend school and ensuring the child receives at least some modest food each day. This is only one of the small steps and imaginative thinking that along with so much effort, can and does, make a difference.

Abra Wagdi

Ajman, United Arab Emirates

MDG 8 – DEVELOP A GLOBAL PARTNERSHIP FOR DEVELOPMENT

A significant question which arises now and needs to be addressed is: "What happens after 2015?" Will the program be aborted and deemed overzealous with optimistic but unrealistic slogans like "Make Poverty History" or will it nevertheless be continued beyond 2015 with the adoption of further necessary targets like global partnership in gradual replacement of fossil fuels with renewable energy?

Catherine Conlon

Cork, Ireland

MDG 5 – IMPROVE MATERNAL HEALTH

... How reliable are these figures? Many of the developing countries have significant gaps in data on population and vital statistics. Census and vital statistics data is frequently incomplete, inaccurate, unreliable and less than timely. Facility-based population services may improve data. But many women die in childbirth, without any record of having attended at a clinical facility. Frequently, women die in childbirth in rural areas with the help of an inexperienced and untrained Traditional Birth Attendant (TBA). Their death is not registered, not recorded.

Colm Turner

Limerick, Ireland

MDG 7 – ENSURE ENVIRONMENTAL SUSTAINABILITY

... Local initiatives should receive much praise for their ingenuity and deserve our attention and investment. A rain harvest system that delivers clean drinking water has been a resounding success. First pioneered in small communities of India and South Africa, the water is disinfected by running it under an Ultraviolet light. The system, when operational, can provide ten litres of water daily to every individual, comfortably above the World Health Organisation estimate for basic daily water requirements of seven litres. Cheap and easy to construct, the initiative has been adopted by numerous communities around the globe both in the developed and developing world.

Peter McCarron

Derry, Northern Ireland

MDG 1 – ERADICATE EXTREME POVERTY AND HUNGER

... We know we can do it. The End Poverty 2015 website suggests that $50 billion in extra aid each year could be enough to meet all the goals. I get angry because I know that much more than this is wasted every year.... I will finish with a few questions. Will people still be starving to death in 2110? In what year will starvation, like small pox finally be consigned to the list of historical causes of death? When will students look back with disbelief that anyone could actually die from hunger on such a resource rich planet?

Tom Smith

Tipperary, Ireland

MDG 8 – DEVELOP A GLOBAL PARTNERSHIP FOR DEVELOPMENT

It's my hope that the last few minutes have left you feeling discomfort and unease. I have been purposefully provocative with this short address, your Excellencies, and, while it would have been easy to come up here and expound how magnanimous we are for setting admirable goals, I feel it is more productive to use the time to gauge where we are going wrong so that we can correct our actions. I wish to convey to you my concerns that, rather than being coherent goals for the betterment of our world, the Millennium Development Goals are inherently flawed instruments which maintain the status quo. Luckily, we can correct this as we strive for the eradication of hunger and poverty.

Irene Chikumbo

Harare, Zimbabwe

MDG 6 – COMBAT HIV/AIDS, MALARIA AND OTHER DISEASES

HIV/AIDS has no boundaries. Aubrey Hooks said: "AIDS knows no race, economic class, or nationality. It takes no sides in political conflict. It is blind to differences of ethnicity and age. In short, it kills without prejudice. Therefore, so too must we form our armies against AIDS across political, national, racial, and religious lines." We must, together take full responsibility and depend less on the developed countries.

Appendix

List of Participating Schools

School/College University	City/Town	Area/County/State	Country
Ajman University	Ajman		United Arab Emirates
Al-Burkan Grammar School	Birmingham	West Midlands	England
Alton Convent School	Ellisfield	Hampshire	England
American University of Sharjah			United Arab Emirates
Aquinas Grammar School	Belfast	Co Antrim	Northern Ireland
Ard Scoil Mhuire	Ballinasloe	Co Galway	Ireland
Asia Pacific College	Manila		Philippines
Bailieboro Community School	Bailieboro	Co Cavan	Ireland
Ballincollig Community School	Ballincollig	Co Cork	Ireland
Ballyfermot College of Further Education	Lucan	Co Dublin	Ireland
Bandon Grammar School	Bandon	Co Cork	Ireland
Bandung Institute of Technology	Jakarta		Philippines
Bethel Middle School	Bethel	Connecticut	USA
Birla Institute of Technology and Science	Tenkasi	Tirunelveli District	India
Borel Middle School	San Mateo	California	USA

Boston University	Boston	Massachusetts	USA
Bournemouth Collegiate School	Bournemouth	Dorset	England
Breifne College	Drumard	Co Cavan	Ireland
Bronx International High School	Bronx	New York	USA
Cary Academy	Cary	North Carolina	USA
Catoctin High School	Thurmont	Maryland	USA
Challney High School for Girls	Luton	Bedfordshire	England
Christ King Girls Secondary School	Rochestown	Co Cork	Ireland
Clonburris National School	Clondalkin	Co Dublin	Ireland
Colaiste Bride	Enniscorthy	Co Wexford	Ireland
Colaiste Chroí Mhuire	Carraroe	Co Galway	Ireland
Coláiste Íde	An Daingean Uí Chúis	Co Kerry	Ireland
Colaiste Mhuire	Askeaton	Co Limerick	Ireland
Colaiste na Toirbhirte	Bandon	Co Cork	Ireland
Colaiste Ris	Dundalk	Co Louth	Ireland
Colaiste Treasa	Mallow	Co Cork	Ireland
Cotswold School	Cheltenham	Gloucestshire	England
Davao del Norte State College	Panabo City	Davao del Norte	Philippines
Davitt College	Castlebar	Co Mayo	Ireland
De La Salle Humanities College	Croxteth	Liverpool	England
Dominican College	Galway	Co Galway	Ireland
Dominican College	Griffith Avenue	Dublin	Ireland
Dominican College	Wicklow Town	Co Wicklow	Ireland

Douglas Community School	Douglas	Co Cork	Ireland
Dover College	Dover	Kent	England
Dr. Kevin M. Hurley Middle School	Seekonk	Massachusetts	USA
Eastern Regional High School	Voorhees	New Jersey	USA
el Mokaouma School	Annaba		Algeria
Falcaragh Community School (PCC)	Falcarragh	Co Donegal	Ireland
Flegg High School	Great Yarmouth	Norfolk	England
Friends School	Lisburn	Co Antrim	Northern Ireland
Glanmire Community College	Glanmire	Co Cork	Ireland
Gothenburg University	Gothenburg		Sweden
Grey Court School	Kingston Vale	London	England
Hawassa University	Hawassa		Ethiopia
Henry Beaufort School	Winchester	Hampshire	England
High School attached to Capital Normal University	Beijing		China
High School	Clonmel	Co Tipperary	Ireland
High School	Terenure	Dublin	Ireland
'Homeschool'	Newberg	Oregon	USA
'Homeschool'	Sacramento	California	USA
'Homeschool'	St. Petersburg	Florida	USA
Indian Springs School	Centreville	Alabama	USA
International School	Meerbusch	Dusseldorf	Germany
International Studies Learning Center	Los Angeles	California	USA

Jadaupur Baghajatin High School	Kolkata	West Bengal	India
John Scottus Senior School	Donnybrook	Dublin	Ireland
John Taylor High School	Staffordshire		England
Joseph Wright College	Alvaston	Derbyshire	England
Kealing Middle School	Austin	Texas	USA
Kingsbridge International High School	Bronx	New York	USA
Kinsale Community College	Kinsale	Co Cork	Ireland
Lady Margaret School	Fulham	London	England
Laurel Hill Coláiste FCJ	Limerick	Co Limerick	Ireland
Lehigh University	Bethlehem	Pennsylvania	USA
Linslade Middle School	Bedfordshire		England
London School of Economics	London		England
London School of Hygiene & Tropical Medicine	London		England
Loreto College	Foxrock	Co Dublin	Ireland
Loreto College	Swords	Co Dublin	Ireland
Loreto Community School	Milford	Co Donegal	Ireland
Loreto Convent Secondary School	Fermoy	Co Cork	Ireland
Loreto Secondary School	Navan	Co Meath	Ireland
Loreto Secondary School	Wexford	Co Wexford	Ireland
Maharaja Sawai Mansingh Vidyalaya	Jaipur		India
Manor House School	Raheny	Dublin	Ireland

Manuel L. Quezon University	Marikina City		Philippines
McNicol Middle School	Miramar	Florida	USA
Mean Scoil Mhuire	Longford	Co Longford	Ireland
Mean Scoil Nua an Leigh Triuigh	Castlegregory	Co Kerry	Ireland
Methodist College	Belfast	Co Antrim	Northern Ireland
Modern Vidya Niketan	New Delhi		India
Monkstown Community School	Newtownabbey	Co Antrim	Northern Ireland
Moorestown High School	Moorestown	New Jersey	USA
Mount St. Michael Secondary School	Claremorris	Co Mayo	Ireland
Mountrath Community School	Mountmellick	Co Laois	Ireland
National University of Computer and Emerging Sciences	Karachi		Pakistan
NYSC	Benue	Imo State	Nigeria
NWFP	Abbotabad		Pakistan
Oathall Community College	Haywards heath	West Sussex	England
Our Lady's Grammar	Newry	Co Down	Northern Ireland
Parkview School	Los Angeles	California	USA
Parrenthorn High School	Manchester		England
Patrician Academy	Mallow	Co Cork	Ireland
Peace Operations Training Institute	Khartoum		Sudan
Pobalscoil Cloich Cheann Fhaola	Falcarragh	Co Donegal	Ireland

Portadown College	Portadown	Co Armagh	Northern Ireland
Prenton High School	Birkenhead	Merseyside	England
Presentation College	Tuam	Co Galway	Ireland
Presentation Secondary School	Mitchelstown	Co Cork	Ireland
Presentation Secondary School	Thurles	Co Tipperary	Ireland
Presentation Secondary School	Tralee	Co Kerry	Ireland
Progress Academy	Cary	North Carolina	USA
Ravenscroft School	Raleigh	North Carolina	USA
Rice College	Ennis	Co Clare	USA
Sacred Heart Secondary School	Clonakilty	Co Cork	Ireland
Saint Raphaelas	Stillorgan	Co Dublin	Ireland
Salesians College	Limerick	Co Limerick	Ireland
Santa Sabina Dominican College	Raheny	Dublin	Ireland
School Without Walls Senior High School	Washington	District of Columbia	USA
Scoil Chuimsitheach Chiarain	Galway	Co Galway	USA
Scoil Damhnait	Westport	Co Mayo	Ireland
Scoil Mhuire	Strokestown	Co Roscommon	Ireland
Sekolah Menengah Kebangsaan Bukit Jelutong	Shah Alam	Selangor	Malaysia
St Augustine School	Westchester	New York	USA
St. Benedict's School	Hanwell	London	England
St. Brigid's National School	Blessington	Co Wicklow	Ireland

St. Catherine's Vocational School	Killybegs	Co Donegal	Ireland
St. Columba's College	Lifford	Co Donegal	Ireland
St. Conleth's College	Ballsbridge	Dublin	Ireland
St. Fintan's	Doon	Co Limerick	Ireland
St. Gerard's	Bray	Co Wicklow	Ireland
St. Joseph of Cluny	Killiney	Co Dublin	Ireland
St. Joseph's Institution			Singapore
St. Kevin's Community College	Adamstown	Dublin	Ireland
St. Macartan's College	Monaghan	Co Monaghan	Ireland
St. Mary's Secondary School	Edenderry	Co Offaly	Ireland
St. Patrick's Academy	Dungannon	Co Tyrone	Northern Ireland
St. Paul's Girls Secondary School	Greenhills	Dublin	Ireland
St. Peter's College	Wexford	Co Wexford	Ireland
St. Thomas Aquinas	Birmingham	West Midlands	England
St. Vincent's School	Glasnevin	Dublin	Ireland
Staten Island Technical High School	Staten Island	New York	USA
Sturbridge Academy	Raleigh	North Carolina	USA
Sutton Grammar School for Boys	Sutton	Surrey	England
Templeogue College CSSp	Templeogue	Dublin	Ireland
Theoretical Lyceum	Vorniceni Village		Moldava
Trevor Day School	New York	New York	USA
Tunku Abdul Rahman College	Selangor		Malaysia

University College Cork	Cork	Co Cork	Ireland
University College Dublin	Belfield	Dublin	Ireland
University of Nairobi	Nairobi		Kenya
University of the Philippines	Manila		Philippines
University of Port Harcourt	Port Harcourt		Nigeria
University Utara Malaysia	Gelugor	Palau Pinang	Malaysia
Virginia College	Virginia	Co Cavan	Ireland
Walkersville Middle School	Walkersville	Maryland	USA
Wallace Hall Academy	Dumfries and Galloway		Scotland
Waterpark College	Waterford	Co Waterford	Ireland
Wesley College	Ballinteer	Dublin	Ireland
Winterton Comprehensive	North Lincolnshire		England
Witts University	Johannesburg		South Africa
Xavier Institute of Management	Bhubaneswar		India